My Romeo & me

The extraordinary story of Romuald & Mary Heroux

Mary Heroux

Diamond Legacies
your story is your legacy

All rights reserved © Mary Heroux

All images:
Property of the author

Editors:
Brian Crum Ewing
Pauline Clark

Book Design:
Cheryl Antao-Xavier
inourwords2008@gmail.com

Publishing Assistance:
Diamond Legacies
(an imprint of In Our Words Inc.)

ISBN: 978-1-989403-35-8 [paperback]

No part of this publication may be reproduced, distributed, or transmitted in any form or by any means, including photocopying, recording, or other electronic or mechanical methods, without the prior written permission of the author.

Dedication

To my Romeo, my love, my friend,
for our 44 years together, with its ups and downs,
its adventures and excitement.
Always in my thoughts till we meet again,
and never to part.

Introduction

Romeo had lived a very interesting life, a life that he really enjoyed (most of the time), which led him to consider writing an autobiography. He thought about the project much and often, but the closest he ever came to actually writing a book was in 1997. We went to Portugal for a two-month vacation, and Romeo thought the trip would be a good time to try writing his memoir—he would be relaxed, with nothing to do or think about—so he brought along his tape-recorder.

One day, he turned on the machine and started talking. Romeo had said he would like my help with the recording, but after a short time I guess he decided he didn't, or else I was giving him too much help, because he stopped, and we had a lengthy (sometimes quite heated) discussion, mainly about the help I was giving. After we said what we had to say, Romeo went to turn on the recorder to continue, only to realize he hadn't turned it off—the machine had been recording us all the while. He had many chapters for his book that couldn't be used. We had a good laugh, nothing more was done about the book, and Romeo just relaxed for the rest of the holiday.

The biggest difference between Romeo and I was that, while Romeo was a go-getter (always wanting to do more, learn more, take on more challenges), I'm very much the opposite. I tend to take the line of least resistance, to be content with whatever comes. Romeo, however, faced life "head-on." He wasn't easily discouraged. Although there were obstacles in his life that would have brought many people to a halt, he would not be beat; from his youngest days to his oldest, an obstacle was just a challenge to overcome. As a result, his life was full of adventure and remarkable accomplishments. It is for this reason that I, too, think that Romeo's life was worth recording. I feel that if I put something of his life down on paper, you, the reader, will agree.

Contents

CHAPTER 1
Romeo's Childhood /1
Romeo's Mother Dies /5
Romeo Leaves Home /7
Romeo and Norma /9

CHAPTER 2
My Family Roots /21
Move to Ontario /23
Toronto During WWII /25
After the War /27

CHAPTER 3
My Life with Romeo Begins /43
Jackson's Cove /47
Retirement /53
By the Work of His Hands /58
Port Elgin /78

CHAPTER 4
Missions & Work Teams /83
The South Seas and South America /97

CHAPTER 5
Travels /105
Romeo Enjoyed Young People /124
God's Healing Touch /128
God's Amazing Grace /131

CHAPTER 6
Romeo's Passing /133
Memory Lane /135
A Last Word… /145

Acknowledgements /147

Romeo & Mary Heroux

16th May 1975

CHAPTER 1

Romeo's Childhood

Hard Work…
Romeo liked to tell me of his former years. I loved to listen to all his stories, even the second or third time. Romeo had a very interesting life, even though it had been very hard for him while growing up. Romeo's father Charles was very ambitious, and took on many jobs of all kinds, much to the sorrow of the family. He expected much from his family, especially from the boys, far more than should have been demanded from boys their age. When ploughing, etc., had to be done, the boys (mostly Gerrard and Romeo, until the other boys grew older) had to be up real early to feed the horses and be ready to work shortly after sunrise. They put in long hours.

There was a bakeshop (owned and managed, for many years, by the Heroux family), and in the winter season Charles took on the job of supplying stores in other towns, delivering bread and soft-drinks. Both of these products were produced in Ville Marie. Romeo talked of working in the soft-drink factory, where sometimes a bottle wouldn't turn out right, and since he liked soft drinks (crème soda being his favourite), he would drink them. By the end of the day, he would be feeling a little sick.

On delivery runs, Romeo and Gerrard would leave before daylight, with two teams and sleighs loaded with either bread or soft-drinks. It gets very cold in northern Quebec. To make sure the soft-drink bottles didn't freeze and break, a lantern was placed in the middle of the load; the bottles were then covered with a tarp, or probably a horse blanket. It didn't matter if the bread froze. The boys would bring sandwiches to eat on the trip. Romeo said sometimes they would make a fire and thaw the sandwiches, which would be frozen by lunch time.

One town, Lorrainville, was close enough for them to make the trip in one day. The other town, Laverlochere, took two days. The boys would stop at a farm, halfway into the journey, to spend the night. Charles had arranged that, besides a place to sleep, they got supper, breakfast, and a lunch for the next day. There was also hay and water for the horses. Romeo said it was a good place to stay. The food was good, and he liked waking to the smell of breakfast cooking. Romeo said it was a man—an old bachelor—cooking; he could see him through the crack in the floor. They spent the next night in the town, sleeping again at the old man's place on the way home.

Romeo told of doing other jobs, such as one where he had to take a car across Lake Temiskaming to the Ontario side, where the highway was open, and the owner could drive to southern Ontario. The car was pulled across the frozen lake, with the front wheels on the sleigh. Another job was to deliver a casket with the corpse in it. That was a bit nerve wracking. Romeo said it was worthwhile when he was fed a good lunch – lots of sandwiches and sweets.

Life wasn't easy at home, where there was always lots of work to be done. One of Romeo's jobs was looking after the little chickens, just out of the incubator. He had to make sure the heat was just right, day and night. He didn't like milking; he thought milking was a job for the girls, and always managed to find another job to do. Charles also grew and sold vegetables; they always had a big garden, which produced lots of vegetables. Romeo had to look after the boxes of seedlings, keep them watered. It was also Romeo's job to sell the vegetables, and that was a job he liked. Sometimes he would use some of the money to buy a chocolate bar, a treat they seldom got.

Romeo had a wagon, and he would go door to door in town, selling the vegetables. One day, a man had an old horse he didn't need (and he also wanted a bag of potatoes), and he suggested that Romeo should have a horse and a bigger wagon. A deal was made—the man got the potatoes, and Romeo got the horse. A rather skinny old horse, but Romeo fed him well and put some flesh on his bones. Romeo got a bigger wagon, and his sister Marie Jeanne did a good job painting it so it would advertise the vegetables. Romeo also had two dogs, which he trained to pull his sleigh to school. If kids were extra nice to him, he would give them a ride, or let them use the sleigh at recess.

Regardless of how demanding and hard it was to please his father, Romeo still had great respect for Charles. He always talked of how intelligent Charles was—how he was a hard worker and a good businessman, and very ingenious, always thinking of ways to make life easier. Many good traits of his father were passed on to Romeo, and it showed in his work at Hydro, where, as a manager, he was always trying

Romeo, 16 years old, standing in the sleigh he used for deliveries.

to find ways to make the work easier for his men, or to save time and money on the job.

Speaking of Charles as a good businessman, Romeo was always proud of his father as a jobber. Every fall, Charles would be happy to head to his camp in the bush, where he took out logs for the paper mill. The logs were slid down a chute into the lake, made into a boom, and floated down to the paper mill at Temiskaming. Charles had lots of horses and hired men to work for him. His camp was large and provided food and lodging for the workers. Romeo was happy when, some winters, they would all go to the camp. Romeo's mother was a teacher, so the children didn't miss out on their education.

Romeo liked school; he wanted to learn and be at the head of his class. The rule was the better you did, the farther forward you sat. Romeo said he would almost get to the front, but then his father would need to keep him home for work—anything that had to be done, both summer and

Below: At a bush camp in 1928: Romeo (2 years) holds his mother Valeda's hand. His sisters (l to r) Marie-Jeane (4 years) and Aline Heroux (3 years)

winter. Charles thought education wasn't necessary; just learn how to work hard. Romeo was embarrassed one time (after missing a few days of school) when the teacher said, "Why weren't you at school? Were you picking potatoes?" This was in the middle of winter. Romeo said because of remarks like this he got teased a lot.

Romeo's Mother Dies

Romeo talked a lot of his mother Valeda. To listen to Romeo, I believe she must have been the most loved woman in his life. How very sad it was when she died, at the young age of 35, while giving birth. The baby died a few months later. Romeo was only 9 years old when Valeda died. The youngest child, Claude, was 2 years old. The eldest, Marie Jeanne, was 13; she thought she could be "mother" and take care of the family of seven, but this didn't happen. A housekeeper named Evelyn, with two children, moved in to help out, and, soon after, she and Charles were married.

Below: Romeo's mother Valeda with her students

The extended Heroux family pose for an impressive photo. (l to r) Girard, Marie Jeanne, Agathe, Thérèse, Claude, Charles, Monique, Evelyn, Florent, Aline, Réal and Romeo.

The Heroux children weren't too happy with the marriage of Charles to Evelyn: they didn't want a new mother and more siblings. Romeo especially wasn't happy. He had been the oldest boy, and now Gerrard, five years older, was taking his place. Romeo thought Gerrard was a brat, but over the years, however, Romeo's feelings changed, and he spoke highly of Gerrard—how smart he was, and that he was a very good farmer. The Heroux family grew from seven children—Marie Jeanne, Aline, Romuald (Romeo), Real, Florent, Agathe and Claude—to nine, with the addition of Gerrard and Therese. Charles and Evelyn were also blessed with a baby girl, Monique, bringing the family to ten.

Evelyn decided ten children were too many to look after by herself, so Charles had to quit his job in the bush. He wasn't happy about the decision. Romeo said that when fall came, his dad would long to be going to his camp in the bush.

Romeo and Evelyn, his stepmother.

Romeo Leaves Home

By sixteen, Romeo had had enough of living at home, and working on the farm, so he made up his mind to leave, and he did. After a parade on St. John the Baptist Day, as soon as it was dark enough that no one would see them leave, Romeo and a friend started walking down the highway, with Temiskaming in mind. After walking for some time, they came to a boarding house. Romeo's friend knew of it, and since the door wasn't locked, they went in. They were very quiet, and after checking some of the bedrooms they found one not occupied. They slept for a while but made sure they were out before anyone was up. Romeo left twenty-five cents of the little money he had, on the dresser. Back on the road, they were given a ride by a trucker. The trucker felt sorry for them when he found out they hadn't eaten for some time, took them to a restaurant, and paid for their food. Romeo almost choked on his food when he heard someone say, "Romuald Heroux, your father is looking for you."

At home Romeo had been missed in the morning. Mary Jeanne told Romeo later of how sad they had all been to hear he had left. His father guessed what was going on, and he and Evelyn went to pick him up. When Charles asked Romeo if he wanted to come home,

Romeo wears the new suit he "borrowed" from his friend. His friend, of course, had no idea that he had "lent" his brand-new suit to Romeo!

the answer was no. Charles was well acquainted with the store owner in Temiskaming. Charles took Romeo there, and by the afternoon Romeo was working in the store. Temiskaming is on the border of Quebec and Ontario and the language in the store was all English. It was a challenge for Romeo, but he always wanted to learn English, and this was a good way to start. The friend he started with "chickened out" and went home.

Romeo had other jobs, besides being a clerk in the store: he delivered groceries, and the express post—mail and parcels—from the railway station. One day a parcel for a friend came in the post. Romeo already knew that it was a suit his friend had ordered, and since the friend wasn't home when Romeo went to deliver it, he decided to have some fun with it. He took the parcel home, opened it, and tried on the suit. Romeo thought he looked pretty handsome (the suit fit him well, and looked good on him), so he had his picture taken. The next day, he rewrapped the parcel and delivered it to his friend.

L: Romeo and Norma Heroux.
R: Romeo and Norma with their children, John and Anne Marie

Romeo and Norma

Romeo was in his late teens, and delivering coal, when he met Norma, his wife-to-be. Romeo said that, when they first met, he was having difficulty remembering Norma's name. He was learning English, and to help him with his studies he read the comics. One of these comics was Maggie & Jiggs, and since he couldn't remember Norma's name, he called her "Maggie," and in return, Norma called Romeo "Jiggs." The name Maggie disappeared but Jiggs carried on. From then on, Romeo was called Jiggs, or Uncle Jigs, by Norma's family. Romuald is Romeo's proper name, but when he worked for Ontario Hydro the men couldn't pronounce Romuald, or found it too hard to say, so they shortened it to Romeo.

Romeo wondered what Norma saw in him, just a truck driver, and usually black from the coal. Norma was secretary for the "big wig" at the mill; she was good at her work, very fast on the typewriter and at taking shorthand. Not only was she well-educated, but she was also pretty, with a shape that could draw a whistle. They were married in September of 1947. Life was good, but not always: they lost their first baby, Marie, at ten months old, from leukemia. There was nothing the hospital could do for the child, so she was taken home. Romeo spoke of how sad it was to come home from work and see Marie grow a little weaker each day. A few weeks after the heartbreaking diagnosis, the child died.

Life went on, and things got better when John was born, in November of 1950; the new baby eased their minds after losing little Marie. And then, in June of 1953, Anne Marie was born.

After Norma and Romeo were married, Norma thought Romeo could do better than driving a truck for a living, and he started to work for Ontario Hydro in 1949. It was a career that lasted until he retired in 1982, and it took him all over northern Ontario, to many different work sites, staying at each location for two or three years. It meant a lot of moves. Some men would live in the work colony, while their family remained at home, but this kind of life was not for Norma and Romeo. Norma told Romeo that, even though she knew life in a trailer was tough, she and the children would follow him wherever he had to go. This pleased him, because life at a camp without his family would have been miserable for Romeo. It was a very rugged lifestyle: In the winter it was very cold—in the morning the bed coverings might be frozen to the trailer wall; sometimes the oil would get so thick from the cold it wouldn't flow into the furnace. In the spring and summer, the mosquitoes and blackflies were almost unbearable.

There was one other thing that Norma was concerned about. Quite often the only transportation to and from the Hydro site would be by rail; Norma would watch the train go north one day, and not return south until the next day. Norma always hoped all would go well, with no emergency, until the train came her way again. This worry, plus being confined to the small trailer with nothing to do, alone all day, with the children at school, was too much for her. Something had to be done. Since Norma was well-trained as a secretary, Hydro soon found her a job in the office. Norma was fine after that, for she liked to work.

Romeo was always proud of Hydro. He said the company always did the best for their employees, to keep them happy and content, to make their life a joy while living in the bush.

Listening to John and Anne Marie, Romeo also did his best to make their life as pleasant and happy as possible. Each time, after every move to a new location, Romeo always built a lean-to, making a room for a pool-table and other things. John was happy with the lean-to, and when it wasn't being used for a round of pool, the pool-table was used for homework, or as a place to play games.

Romeo believed in "a place for everything and everything in its place." He told me you couldn't expect a place to be tidy if there wasn't a place for children to hang their clothes, especially in the winter. Also, a place was needed for books, games, all the things children need for entertainment. Romeo also used this approach while on the job—he called it "good housekeeping," an important part of his work routine.

For Anne Marie's amusement, he made her a playhouse. Anne Marie was overjoyed with it, and she spent many happy hours in it. Anne Marie

Above left: John and Anne Marie at Christmas. Right: John's confirmation. Below: Weddings of Romeo's children: Left, John to Maureen Maloney on April 7, 1984, in Vancouver B.C. and Anne Marie to Doug Bell on July 22, 1992 in Owen Sound, Ontario.

Above: John (Romeo's son) and his wife, Maureen, prepare to enjoy a meal with Thérèse and Gilles Adam.

Below L: Daddy's girl. Romeo shares a tender moment with his daughter, Anne Marie. R: Anne Marie and her husband, Doug Bell.

described it to me, and I believe she thought it was "second to none." By her description I believe she was right. The imitation fireplace was made of bricks, with a mantle, and had birch wood in it, looking like firewood ready to be lit. There was a sink, a table and bench, and a picture window, with a flower box that Anne Marie filled with marigolds. The door had a window in it so one could see who was coming. Romeo was pleased with the playhouse, and told me how cute it was, to see the row of little shoes outside on the verandah when Anne Marie was entertaining some friends.

Norma's parents lived in North Bay. Romeo made sure they visited them often, and Norma and the children would spend time there in the Summer holidays. Sometimes it would just be Anne Marie and John spending time with their grandparents.

Romeo worked on many power projects in Northern Ontario: Rapids Des Joachim, Cameron Falls, Iroquois Falls, Little Long Rapids, Manitou Falls, Otter Rapids, Pine Portage, Red Rock Falls, Ear Falls, Harmon Station, Kipling, and Silver Falls. In 1965, Romeo was transferred from the jobs in Northern Ontario to the nuclear power plant in Pickering. What a joy for Norma! They bought a beautiful house in Whitby, and all new furniture. They even hired an interior decorator to place furniture, etc. Seemed like all should be happy, but John often wished for life in the "bush" again; he missed fishing with his dad and other things that just aren't in the city.

Good things, sadly, can also come to an end, and this is what happened. After a short time (possibly two years), Romeo was transferred once more, this time to the power plant at the Bruce, on Lake Huron, and Norma had to leave her beautiful house. They moved to Port Elgin, where the beach and Lake Huron must have made it a little bit attractive. They moved into a roomy log house, right on the water. The road wasn't kept open in the winter; they had to use a snowmobile to get to where the car was parked, and Anne Marie used a snowmobile to go to school—she must have been the envy of many of the other students. By this time John had started university in Waterloo, and, since Norma had worked in the Hydro office while up north, she was given another job in the organization, at the Bruce plant.

Norma didn't have the best of health (she had a problem with high blood pressure), and sadness touched the family once again, in 1970, when Norma suffered a stroke which affected her mobility, speech, and memory. It was a very sad time for them all. Anne Marie told me, "It was like I didn't depend on my Mom anymore, she depended on me." Norma wasn't angry about her condition; she was always in a good mood. An Occupational Therapist taught her how to work with one hand and also suggested tools they could get to help her, such as a tool that held a potato firmly so it could be peeled with one hand. Norma got to the point where she could do quite a few things around the house. This was probably good for her, giving her the opportunity to feel more useful.

Romeo asked to work the night shift, so he could be with Norma while Anne Marie was in school. Often, Romeo would take Norma for a drive, or they would just park by the water.

Romeo said these times were very special. After Norma's stroke their log house by the water wasn't convenient for Norma, so they had moved away from the lake.

The Heroux siblings in 2015. (l - r) Monique, Romeo, Marie Jeanne, Agathe, Claude and Thérése. (Réal is not present for the picture).

Once again, Romeo's good attitude proved helpful: In a bad situation, do the best you can and get on with life. Listening to him, Norma had the same attitude; regardless of the situation they had lots of laughs. One day, he and Norma had macaroni and cheese for the evening meal. After eating, while putting away the leftovers, Romeo mentioned that the macaroni would do for lunch. Norma was able to make Romeo's lunches, and when Romeo opened his lunch box that night, much to his dismay, he found macaroni sandwiches. Norma was laughing while she waited for Romeo to come home, because, after he left for work, she realized her mistake – Romeo had wanted the macaroni leftovers for lunch the next day, not for his lunch that night.

The Measure of a Man…
In 1972, Norma and Romeo's 25th Wedding Anniversary was coming up, and Romeo had bought Norma a silver tea service for the occasion. But, the night before the anniversary, there was sad news—Norma had passed away. It was a very sad and hard time for them all. Romeo was really broken up over Norma's death; he shed a lot of tears over it, and the memories he felt for his mother and his little daughter were also making him sad. When he spoke of these times to me, later on, as we were getting to know each other, it was the depth of his feelings, of all this love he had, that appealed to me.

Feeling completely lost without Norma, Romeo turned to alcohol to drown his sorrows. He began missing too much work, and when he did go to work, he wasn't always in "good shape," because he had been drinking too much. Romeo knew Hydro wouldn't put up with this change in him and that he might lose his job. He realized he had to do something about his behaviour. Romeo was strong and determined: if he decided to do something he wouldn't give up until he did it. With the help of God (Romeo believed in prayer), he gave up cigarettes and alcohol completely. He wouldn't even drink a glass of wine to toast at weddings, for fear he would start drinking again. Romeo always thanked God for helping him get over his drinking problem, and for being with him through this very sad time in his life. He never forgot how God was always there, with him, when there were problems to solve at work. Many times, he had prayed to God for help, and many times the problem had been solved.

His willpower to give up alcohol was acknowledged later, at his retirement party—one of the speeches given was what Romeo had been like to work with when he was drinking, and the improvement when he stopped. Two other wives at the party told me they wished their husbands would follow Romeo's example. He was presented with a bottle of whiskey that had been encased in a sealed wooden box, with a small, round opening protected by bars. He was also presented with a clock, to which he responded, "A clock, the last thing I need now!" This brought a laugh, as everyone knew that time was a priority with Romeo—everything had to be done on time—except now, after he had retired.

Romeo enjoyed his work at Hydro. He found everything interesting and challenging. But it wasn't always good. Once, when Romeo was interviewing a man for a job, he thought by the man's looks that he had a drinking problem. Romeo asked the man if he did, and the man admitted he had difficulty with alcohol, but he said that he was trying to quit and was going to Alcoholics Anonymous for help. Romeo told him he would help him any way he could, and that he would be put on a shift that would allow him to continue going to AA for help. Romeo hired the man, but he wasn't doing well; he would come to work drunk sometimes. Romeo told him not to come to work if he had been drinking, but it didn't do any good. After Romeo warned him (as many times as he was allowed), he told the man

One of the parting gifts Romeo received when he retired from Ontario Hydro was a bottle of whiskey encased within a barred box. It was given in recognition of him having successfully quit drinking.

that he would have to let him go. The man pleaded for his job, claiming that his wife would leave him if he lost this job. Romeo said he was sorry but there was nothing more he could do. The man went home and shot himself. Romeo really felt bad, but if there had been an accident caused by someone who had been drinking, Romeo would have been in the wrong.

Romeo was strict with the men. He expected good work, because they were getting good pay. Some men resented this attitude and thought Romeo hard to work for. Others liked his method and said that when they worked for Romeo, they always knew exactly what they were to do, and how they were to do it. He was strict but always fair, always looking for ways to better the job and make the work easier for the men. Romeo could always notice men who were hard workers, not just there for a pay cheque, and he let them know how much he appreciated them.

Regardless of how much Romeo enjoyed his work with Hydro there were always problems to solve (some small, some big), and he never took any of them lightly. Romeo would come home from work, sometimes thinking of something that would have to be worked out the next day, and he would be expected to solve it. One way or another, the problems would work out okay. Once again, Romeo would give God the credit, for he had a strong belief in God and that He definitely answers prayers.

Romeo was very strict on what he called "good housekeeping." The areas where men were working had to be neat—no lumber crisscrossed, but always piled neat so no one would trip. Boards with nails in them were never left lying around—either the nails were removed, or the boards were turned over, with nails toward the floor. Because of his good work habits, Romeo received two safety awards recognizing a total of 24 years of no accidents among his men that resulted in lost work time.

Anne Marie, Romeo's daughter worked for Ontario Hydro until she developed multiple sclerosis. Finally she was bedridden. Anne Marie has a great attitude, never felt sorry for herself, great sense of humour, interested in people, a warm smile and always a "I'm fine" reply. A delight to visit her.

Doug Bell, Romeo's son-in-law, taught Marine Navigation at Georgian College in Owen Sound for 35 years, from 1974 to 2009 then part time after retirement.

Below: Doug at the controls of a simulator with a merchant marine officer. He taught marine students who might sail anywhere in the world. They are mostly in our Great Lakes. The Toronto skyline is in the background.

Romeo's son, John, had some experience in construction at Bruce G.S. and then in community health services mostly on the west coast. From ambulance services to community mental health, his experience is varied. From 1999 to 2012, he held a succession of senior administrative positions with manufacturers of medical devices and technologies (MDMI Tech) in Richmond, B.C.

John's wife, Maureen (below) also has a distinguished career in the medical field. Currently, she is part of a mobile vaccination team in southeastern B.C.

CHAPTER 2

My Family Roots

Mary's Life...
Compared to Romeo's life, my life was pretty ordinary, but, as they say, everyone has a story, so I'll share some of my fifty years of life, before I met Romeo.

My father, Hans Christian Hansen, was born in Denmark, November 4, 1867. In his early 20's he came to America, to New York. America was thought of then as a "new land," with lots of promise. He worked for the Chicago Pacific Railway, and also farmed. In 1873, because of good reports from his uncle Carl Jensen in Canada, Hans moved to the region that would become (in 1905) the province of Saskatchewan.

Dad staked out a claim for half of a section of land (320 acres), which after three years, if he proved himself a good steward by erecting a barn and a house, and by having a number of acres producing a crop, would become his, free of charge. He later bought a further quarter-section of land, which increased the farm to 480 acres.

My mother, Anna Catherine Scheuermann, was born near Durham, Ontario, on November 16, 1893. Hans married Catherine (known as Kate) in 1913. My father was thrilled to marry my mother; he was 46 years old, and he thought that he would probably remain a bachelor all his life. To now be able to raise children brought him even more joy. Eight children were born, but, sadly, my brother's twin was stillborn, which made for a family of seven: Christina, Victor, Anna, Gertrude, Mary, Carl, and Margaret.

Dust Storms and Bennet Wagons…

The times were very prosperous for a number of years, till the late '20's, early '30's, when the crops started to fail. Grasshoppers were an occasional threat (they came in large swarms, eating everything in their path), but a major cause of the failures was a lack of rain. Without rain the soil in the fields dried up, and when the winds were strong, there would be dust storms. Whenever you saw a dark cloud on the horizon you knew it was a dust storm; if we were walking home from school and saw one approaching, we would lie face-down in a ditch until the clouds of dust passed over. At home, any clothes on the clothesline were quickly brought indoors, and you would make sure all the windows were tightly closed, but even if they were closed you would still get a layer of dust. We were luckier than some because we had a good well (which also supplied some of the neighbours), plus there was a slough which almost dried up in the summer. It provided pasture for the livestock in the summer and hay for the winter months.

These conditions continued for almost ten years, and as the situation grew worse, hardships increased. Dad had a car, a Model-T, but they say he never really got used to driving it. My mother, however, had no such problem—adventuresome, ready for anything, she was always young at heart and full of fun. The chance to drive the car must have been a real thrill, so Mom would drive to town to take the cream to the railway station. On one such occasion, she didn't hit the brakes fast enough, and the car ran into the station platform. Mom heard one of the men standing nearby, watching her as she drove up, say, "That will stop her."

The use of cars came to an end though, as no one could afford gas. Some cars were cut in half, stripped of their engine, and had a tongue attached so they could be pulled by horses. Since the Prime Minister at that time was Richard Bennet, these became known as Bennet Carts or

Bennet Wagons. Grains like barley, etc., were boiled to brew a substitute for coffee, and they called it Bennet Coffee. I was too young to drink coffee, but people would say it was pretty good.

Move to Ontario

Leaving the Homestead…
Conditions became so bad in Saskatchewan that practically every family was relying on relief payments (probably what is now called Welfare) to get by; it was $10 a month. To ease the financial burden, the government was pleased to move anyone out of the province, go East or West: you were provided with two box cars, free of charge, to carry your possessions. Harry, my brother-in-law, said goodbye to his wife (my sister Christina) and left for Ontario, riding in freight cars, which was allowed because people couldn't afford the fare.

Harry got a job that paid $1 a day for road work, using pick and shovel, and by the end of a year we received word that he had rented a place for him and his wife to live. Since Christina would be travelling with two small children, Mother didn't want her to make the bus trip alone, so she decided to go with her. She also took my brother, 9-year-old Carl, and my sister Margaret, who was 5 years old.

My father was lonely without Mother and kept writing to find out when she was coming home. I think Mother had had enough of Saskatchewan, and I don't think she had any intention of returning, so Dad left for Ontario. It was hard for Dad to leave his "homestead" that he loved, and I think he wished either Vic or Carl would take it over, but that never happened. In 1937 it was decided that the rest of us would join them.

With both parents already in Ontario, the task of moving our property and possessions was left up to us: Vic (20), Anna (18), Gertrude (16), and me, Mary (14). The railway station was at the village of Bemerside, eight miles away. We had good neighbours who helped us with wagons for the furniture and farm machinery, and people on horseback came to herd the cattle and horses. Since there was no way to sell anything, we had to take it all. That included turkeys (some of which we sold while stopped at a railway station in northern Ontario), but the chickens we had were killed by Vic and preserved in jars by Ann and Gertrude, for our food on the train. One of our neighbours, a lady, made a large batch of bread for us, and we also had a huge box of puffed wheat. We had lots of milk—we just had to squeeze it out. The trip to Ontario took seven days, and our food supplies lasted all the way; we were enjoying them, even on the seventh day.

My parents, Hans and Catherine Hansen, on their 50th Wedding Anniversary, taken from a portrait that hangs on my wall. If you look closely at the image, you can see my reflection in the glass of the picture frame.

Mary Heroux

Toronto During WWII

In the fall of 1939, Ann, Gert, and I went to St. Catharines to pick fruit—peaches, pears, and tomatoes. We had fun and got 25 cents an hour. The next spring, I went back and worked on grape vines, but by 1940, we three sisters were in Toronto. Anna worked for a friend who owned a beauty salon, and Gert and I worked at odd jobs (one job was serving gas at Joy Oil gas stations, till gas was rationed and some stations were closed) while at the same time trying to get factory work, making guns, etc., for the war. Because Mother's maiden name was German (Scheuermann), they wouldn't hire us—we were considered a security risk. We finally did get jobs working in a factory (Canadian Elevators, which had changed from making elevators to making fog guns), but only because we changed the Germanic spelling of Mother's name to Sherman.

Gert had a good job. She was taught how to sharpen tools, and she was good at it, and had a pleasant boss. I, along with four or five other girls, sat at a table filing or scraping the burrs off of the gun parts. I wasn't happy with that, so I quit. I found work in a factory where I made small parts for airplanes made out of aluminum. I worked on a lathe, doing precision work, which made it very interesting. A micrometer was used to measure the parts; they had to be within a thousandth of an inch. I liked the job, it wasn't monotonous and I didn't mind working overtime, which happened quite often.

Things were very different in Toronto during the war. There was an overflow of people coming to the city to work. This consisted mostly of women; men who didn't have a business beneficial to the war, or a farm to look after, were enlisted in the services. Since all these people had to have a place to live, anyone who had a room or two in their house to spare would rent them out to lodgers. That was the case with Gert and I; we were paying $2 a week for one room and the use of the family bathroom. Our room consisted of a pull-out couch (which became our bed at night), a table, two chairs, and a two-burner hotplate set on two wooden orange-crates. We used the dividers in the crates as shelves for the few dishes, etc., that we needed. Later, Ann left her job at the beauty salon, our cousin Mary Scheuermann came from Saskatchewan, and the four of us lived together. For $4 a week we shared one large room, a small bedroom, and a bathroom, which was down the hall.

We four got along well and had lots of fun. It cost 35 cents for admission to most of the movie theatres (prices were low at that time), but the two classy ones—Sheas and Lowes—cost 60 cents. To roller-skate was 35 cents, which included renting skates. Sunday morning saw us in church, and always with a hat—a rule for those days: you didn't go to church without a hat. Men always took their hats off when they entered any doors. We went often to Maple Leaf Gardens on Carlton Street. Not sure of the price, but it was probably 50 cents. We enjoyed watching figure skating, the three-ring circus, Roy Rogers and Gene Autry, etc. Mary and I even went to a hockey game. Neither of us were really interested in hockey, but Toronto was playing Saskatchewan, and I think Mary was lonely for her home province. I think Saskatchewan had only one fan, but that one was heard, because when Saskatchewan scored a goal Mary rose to her feet and went off like a siren!

Mary in 1946, while working at the Goodyear factory in Toronto.

After the War

In 1945, with the war over, our cousin Mary Scheuermann (who had come to Toronto for work and had been sharing our rented lodgings) went back to Saskatchewan. My sister Anna got married. Gert and I stayed in Toronto. All the "war factories" went back to their original production. Gert and I worked at Campbell Soup, and for Goodyear. During the war, my wage had been 54 cents an hour; after the war, at Goodyear, we were getting $1.05 per hour (Romeo and I figured out he was probably getting the same wage when he first started working for Hydro).

At Goodyear I worked at a machine, making 'Life Guard' tubes —not the kind of tubes used for rescues at the beach, but the ones used in tires. These tubes had an extra section, which also held air, that worked as a safety device: if you had a "blow-out" while driving, the extra air kept the tire okay until you could stop the car. There were three other girls making Life Guard tubes—Joey, Norma, and Mildred "Millie" Farrell. Millie was a lot of fun to be with, and we became very good friends. She was slim and tall and had a very positive attitude. Our relationship remained strong, even after the end of the war.

Marriage to Hugh...

While working at Goodyear, I met Hugh McCulloch, the man who would become my husband; he worked in the "hot room," where the Life Guard tubes were cured. He had served 4 years in the Air Force in England during World War II. His sister Mary served there as well, as a nurse. Their brother Donald joined the Air Force, but didn't get overseas; after earning his wings, he was stationed in Nova Scotia, as a flying instructor.)

Farm Life on the 10th of Bruce...

After our marriage, we didn't stay in Toronto long. We both liked country life, so in 1948 we decided to buy a farm. The Veterans' Land Act (passed in 1942) was good to servicemen, helping them get settled in whatever livelihood they chose. When we found a farm that we wanted to buy, south of Port Elgin (a hundred acres, for $5000), we only had to put down $500, and the rest was paid for with an interest-free loan, to be paid back within twenty years. This we bought in 1950. Hugh also received $1200.00 from the VLA (Veterans' Land Act) for livestock and implements. The previous owner of our farm had an auction sale, which made a great opportunity for Hugh and me. Hugh bought the team of horses, some cows, the hay in the mow, the bin of oats, and some farm implements. Household items were also sold. I was so pleased to buy the beautiful range. The enamel on it was cream colour with not one chip. It looked brand new. We were pleased with our purchases!

Where we lived in Bruce County and farther south along the shores of Lake Huron, it's known as the snow belt. In the early 60's we had a record snowstorm. Everything was brought to a halt; all roads were closed. Hugh was working for the Bruce nuclear power station at that time. Everyone was trapped. When highway 21 was opened up, Hugh still couldn't get home as all the concession roads were blocked. Hugh stayed in the Town and Country Motel—situated on the highway between concessions #8 and #10—so he could still go to work. Because the snow was so deep

L: Hugh and Donald McCulloch
R: Mary and Hugh McCulloch, 29 December, 1948

on the concession roads, the snow plough couldn't push it away. A snow blower had to be brought from Toronto to blow out the snow. There were lots of roads to be opened and it was two weeks before our road—the 10th concession of Bruce Township—was opened. The children and I were getting low on food, so Hugh bought a toboggan and some groceries and managed to walk the mile and a half, pulling the toboggan to the farm. It wasn't easy; sometimes he was wading in snow almost to his hips! Then he had to be back to the motel and ready for work the next morning. Although farming has its challenges, we liked the country life and thought it was a great place for the children to grow up.

Living so close to the beaches of Lake Huron brings back a flood of happy summer memories. One of those memories is all about the Joneses' cottages. Our neighbours, the Jones family, had cottages on Lake Huron, about three miles away, which they rented, and because I helped clean them in the spring, etc., we often got to use them. It was also good advertising for their business to have a cottage occupied in the slack times.

The Move to Port Elgin…
A house fire in 1967 helped us make the decision to move to Port Elgin in January 1968, to stay with Dad McCulloch, who had Alzheimer's and needed someone to be with him. Aunt Mary (Dad's sister), who was living with him, decided it was too much work for her and wanted to move out. Throughout his life Dad had made it known that he never wanted to be placed in a nursing home, and with his mind as it was, it wouldn't have been good to move him into the homes of the other siblings, so we moved in with him. We all loved him; he was a special person in all our lives, and it was wonderful that the young ones had the opportunity to know their grandpa so well.

It was a cold day in November when the fire happened. A neighbour, Lloyd Brown, was driving by our place and saw smoke coming out of the house. Lloyd phoned the fire department. I was working in the barn at the tobacco farm. We were grading the tobacco leaves and putting them in bales ready to sell, when Irene Enns, the farmer's wife, came to the barn to tell me our house was on fire. By the time I got home there were lots of neighbours there, besides the fire truck, and smoke was billowing out of the house. It was a sad sight, a shock for the children as they got off the bus from school. I phoned Hugh, who was working in Toronto, and he said he would be home as soon as possible.

After the fire was put out, we learned that most of the damage was from the smoke, and that the house could be repaired. Our dear neighbours, Guna and Wolfgang Webber, who lived just down the road from us and were going away for the weekend, offered us their house for the next two days. It was wonderful of them to do that for us, because it solved my problem—I had no idea where we would go that night. When Hugh joined us that evening, we were happy to all be together, and thankful that the fire hadn't started at night. It might have been a very different story. As for the fire in our house, neither we nor the man from the fire insurance company ever found out the cause.

Working on the Tobacco Farm...

The soil around Port Elgin was very suitable for growing tobacco, and there were quite a few tobacco farms. Many of these farms changed their crop, however, when tobacco became less popular. The negative outlook on these farms came when it was brought to light that tobacco was bad for one's health. On the other hand, the positive side for the tobacco farms, was that they provided jobs for many people.

The farmer would hire two or three men for the full season; the rest of the workers would be local people, hired just when needed. I took advantage of this, because we could always use extra money, and I liked working outside. Considering the wages paid in the '60's and early '70's for seasonal work, it was good pay at $1 an hour. Better than 50 cents an hour for painting, wallpapering, or cleaning in a house, which I often did. Plus, having enjoyed being home for almost two months, it wasn't a hardship to go back to work again, especially when you knew it would only be for a month, or a little more.

I had started working at Peter Enns' tobacco farm before we moved to Port Elgin. I began at the beginning of the season, in the green house, (pulling plants to be planted in the field), and worked all summer, until the tobacco was harvested, and the kilns were all filled. When the leaves were dry in the kilns, which took seven days, the kilns were emptied, and the leaves were stored in a barn. The kiln was ready to be filled again; they were filled many times. There were seven kilns, so we got one day off before we could start filling them again. It was crucial to keep the kilns full and the job done as there was a short time period between when the leaves were ready for harvest and the possibility of an early frost. The leaves would be of no use if they were touched by frost. To make sure he had full help at this important time, Pete paid an extra dollar a day to workers who were there every day during the harvest.

The machine used for harvesting was high enough to straddle the plants without injuring the top. There were two seats, one on each side of the row of plants, and as the machine rolls along the bottom leaves of the plants are pulled off and put into containers called boats. The full boats are taken to tying machines, where the leaves are sewn together and hung-over three-foot sticks and hung in the kiln to dry. The job was hard on the back because workers would be in a cramped position all day. Only when the full boats were being switched out and replaced with empty ones could the harvesters (known as primers) seize an opportunity to get up and stretch their backs.

In late fall, having been home for two months, it wasn't hard to go back to work again for "stripping season". The tobacco leaves were stripped off the sticks they had been sewn onto, graded, and baled, ready for market. It was my job to strip the leaves off the sticks, which was very simple—just cut the thread, and a spinning wheel pulled it from the leaves. Two girls, with our boss Pete, graded the leaves as they moved past them on a conveyor belt. Another man put the leaves in bales. It may sound like a monotonous job, and it would have been, if it weren't for Pete's jokes, and getting us to play word games that helped pass the time.

During the growing season there was a time when the suckers (extra branches) had to be taken off the plants. Another time, the flowers had to be broken off the top. At these important times Pete hired extra people, anyone who wanted to make some money. My kids got in on this; they liked earning some money, for we never gave them an allowance. The work took determination and willpower—they had to keep up with the rest of the workers, as each worked on their own row. Payday was real encouraging, for they got full pay, just like everyone else. Some days they worked by themselves, and they got paid a certain amount for each row they did. Once again, they got a good pay.

A Time of Trouble…

One day, Doug came to work on the farm with me when he was about 12. We were suckering the tobacco plants. When doing this job, there is a juice that comes off the plant that looks and sticks like tar—it doesn't come off without a good scrubbing. We had company that night for supper, and by midnight we were all in bed, tired, and some not so clean (too tired to scrub). Doug fell into bed as he was, and I didn't have the heart to wake him in order to clean up.

We hadn't gone to sleep yet when we heard what sounded like the outside door opening and then closing. I went down to investigate, and there was Doug, sitting on a chair, whimpering; he said his feet hurt. A horrible thought came to me, and when I looked at his wrists, I knew what had happened. Doug was a sleepwalker, and while sleepwalking he had climbed out his bedroom window. Being on the second floor, the ground lower on that side of the house, he would have fallen over 20 feet.

For twenty years the McCulloch family – Mary, Hugh, and their children Pauline, Bonnie, and Doug – called this farm their home.

Both Doug's wrists were broken, and he was getting a lump on his head. We took him to the hospital, and casts were put on his wrists. Since Doug had gone to bed with the "tar" stains still on him, I had a lot of explaining to do: Why was my child so dirty? What kind of a mother are you? Thankfully, Doug came through it okay. He had a mind of his own; with only his fingers and thumbs exposed from the cast, he wouldn't let the nurse dress him, nor would he accept any help from the rest of us at home. Even though Doug talked to Hugh and me on the way to the hospital, he didn't remember anything that happened. The first he remembered was waking up in the hospital, with casts on his wrists.

On another occasion, it was a day at the end of a school year, and the students were having a fun time on a Field Day. One of the sports was discus throwing, and a girl was twirling around, getting up speed to throw the discus. There were lots of students standing nearby, watching. The thought occurred to Pauline—what if the discus slipped out of her hand? The next thing Pauline was aware of, she was lying on her back, and people were looking down at her. It had happened just as Pauline thought, and the discus had hit her in the face. Two of her teeth were damaged, and she had to have five stitches in her upper lip. She still has the scar.

When life is good, everyone happy and healthy, we think we "have it made." Nothing can go wrong. It takes something like the experiences we just went through, to get our attention, and to help us to realize that only by the grace of God are we so blessed; only by the grace of God, that we live in this beautiful country Canada, with all the freedom and all our provisions so amply supplied. May we never forget.

A Time of Laughter…
Thank God, life doesn't only consist of troubled times; there are lots of things that happen that can make us smile, even laugh. On one such instance, it being Halloween time, the teacher was planning a party. She needed treats, so she asked for volunteers to bring some. Bonnie came home from school feeling pretty good about something. After she told me of the teacher's request, she proudly said, "I volunteered to bring candied apples." At that point, I didn't know what to say or do! I did manage

to think, however, before I said anything. And even though I had never made candied apples, and had no idea how they were made, I did find a recipe. They must have been okay. No one got sick. Years later we laughed about it—and Bonnie said I never let her down.

Parents as well as children can have a mind of their own, and when it comes to a "showdown" the parent isn't always right. I found this out the hard way, one day. I had baked and iced a cake. It wasn't for anyone's birthday, or for anything special, just dessert for the family. Shortly after the children came home from school, I saw where someone had used their finger to sample the icing. I asked them who did it, and at the same time was sure I knew who; after all, the girls wouldn't do something like that. It really didn't matter because the cake wasn't for anything special. All I wanted was the truth—who did it?

I said to Doug, "Did you do it?" Doug said no, but in a rather teasing way. I said "Doug, I'm going to find out who did it. If it was you, after denying you did it, you are going to get the yardstick across your behind. If you didn't do it, then you can use the yardstick on me." Judging by the satisfied grin on Doug's face and the guilty look on Pauline's, I knew exactly who was going to get the whacks with the yardstick.

My beautiful children (l to r) Bonnie, Doug, and Pauline. They were good kids.

With a lot of laughing, the penalty was administered. It was a joke all along, but nevertheless it was a good lesson for me; I had accused Doug, without even giving it a thought, or asking the girls if they had done it. Parents like to think they're right but, on those occasions, when they know they are wrong, it's important for them to own up to it.

Millie, Ross, and Scott...
Millie Farrell, my friend from Goodyear, got married to Don Williamson. They remained in Toronto, but she and Don liked to visit us on the farm. It was always special to have a visit with Millie and Don, and, as time went by, their two boys, Ross and Scott. It was sad to learn that life wasn't going so well with Millie and Don, and in time it led to a separation. Millie kept the boys, which was okay when the boys were at school, because she could go to work, but it was a problem when the boys were home for summer holidays. When we heard of the separation and Millie's dilemma with the summer situation, we suggested Ross and Scott spend their summer holidays on the farm with us. The arrangement worked out fine, and they came every summer, for about seven years. There was railway transportation between Toronto and Port Elgin at that time.

My dear friend, Millie Williamson and her boys, Scott (in white) and Ross.

Millie could put the boys on the train, and we would be at the station to meet them. Millie often came on the weekends, which we all enjoyed.

Scott was 6, Ross was 8, and our son Doug was 7, when the two boys first came to stay on the farm. It made life interesting for Doug to have brothers, and what those three boys thought up made life interesting for the rest of us—sometimes a little too interesting! I could probably write a book about my son Doug and Millie's boys. I heard of their adventures, years later; Ross was quite the "mastermind."

Our summers were good. After the house fire and our move into Port Elgin to live with Hugh's dad, the boys continued to come for the summer holidays. Dad McCulloch's house was quite small, and only a part of the basement was finished; the girls slept in a room in the finished section. The unfinished area was quite large, and held the furnace, along with a small wood-burning stove that could be used to heat the house if the power went out. Even partially unfinished, it was quite cozy, and Doug slept there, sharing the space with Ross and Scott, who slept on folding cots. Doug never got over his sleep-walking habit. One night— who knows what he was dreaming of—he got up and tipped over Ross and Scott's cots, sending them all rolling onto the floor.

Sleeping quarters for the boys eventually moved to the tent-trailer which we had parked in our driveway, much to the sorrow of our neighbours, Gladys and Basil Eby, as our houses were quite close together, and the trailer was parked under their bedroom window. When you bring three boys together, you find out that they're not exactly quiet neighbours.

It came to a time when Ross grew out of those fun years; he became an adult and joined the work force. Scott continued to visit. He and Doug started working full time in the tobacco fields, helping with the harvest. It was an easy job for the summer, though the hours were long, and the work was hard on one's back.

Remember Lloyd Brown, who called the fire department? Because of him, our house wasn't a complete loss. We were pleased when his son Larry asked if he could room and board with us while he worked at the *(l to r) Ross, Doug, Scott, and Bonnie, on a trip to Collingwood.*

tobacco farm. Sadly, for poor Gladys and Basil, Larry took Ross's place in the trailer, so there was still as much noise as before! As I said, the house was small, so we had a picnic table on the lawn where we ate our meals. The boys got along well, sometimes too well; every so often I'd have to give a shout out the window to tell them to "tone it down."

We have lots of laughs when me and my adopted "kids" (Ross and Scott) get together and reminisce of days gone by. Pauline and Bruce surprised me, one birthday in my early 90's, when they invited Millie, Ross, and Scott to join us for the celebration at their place. Ross had come all the way from Ottawa on his motorcycle. Scott and Doug are great friends, so I see Scott fairly often. He lives in Sutton and drops by every time Doug comes to visit. Millie, who was one year older than me, was living in a nursing home. I hadn't seen her for a few years, and I hadn't seen Ross since those long-gone summer days, so it was a nice surprise.

West Coast Camping Trip…

It was a dream come true when my three teenagers and I decided to drive to the West Coast, camping along the way. Dad McCulloch had passed away from a stroke two years after we moved in with him so although I was sad along with the rest of the family, it meant that I was free to go. The idea was okay with Hugh, as he didn't have the same feeling for camping, and he also had to work. I've always liked camping, ever since my early days in Saskatchewan, when we would drive thirteen miles by team and wagon to pick Saskatoon berries. We would stay a few days to make the long trip worthwhile, so Mom would pack lots of food and some blankets—oh, the fun of sleeping under the wagon at night! We each had a pail that we hung from a sash tied around our waists so our hands would be free for picking. Large cans (used for storing cream for sale) were brought to store the picked fruit. We were encouraged to pick lots of berries, because they would provide a lot of desserts through the long winter. We ate some of them—fresh, with cream and sugar—and Mom would preserve the rest, so, the "taste" of camping came early for me.

(l to r) Doug, Mary, Pauline, and Bonnie stand for a group photo, just before leaving Port Elgin for their trip to the West Coast.

We were gone for five weeks. Pauline was eighteen and had her driver's license, and she helped me with the driving. We left with $400 and the use of a gas card, which wasn't much money for a five-week vacation across Canada. Restaurants were not an option, but no one complained about the 'Do-It-Yourself' type picnics. Visiting friends and relatives and parking the trailer in their yards helped our budget as well!

We drove all the way, right to Vancouver Island. We also went as far north as the Peace River district, in Alberta, to visit Hugh's brother Don McCulloch and his wife Arnetta, who were beekeepers. Don had a small plane that he used mostly to check his bee yards to see if there were any problems with bears. He took each of us for a plane ride; there was only enough room for one passenger at a time. Needless to say, we enjoyed our visit with them and wished we had planned on spending more time at their place. I think Don and Arnetta were favourites of Pauline, Bonnie, and Doug.

Hugh's family was special to me. I loved Hugh's mother Irene, who was a very caring person, and thoughtful toward everyone. Sadly, she died in her 50's, when Hugh and I were in our second year of marriage. As for Arnetta, I liked her from the moment we first met; we became the best of friends. She left a huge hole in my heart when she passed away. Don was very special to Hugh. Even though Don was younger, Hugh looked up to him and respected him, and wouldn't hesitate to ask him for advice. It was a terrible shock and loss for Hugh when Don was killed in an accident in the bush when he was in his early 70's.

In Camrose, Alberta, we stayed a few days with a favourite niece, Unita, her husband Ivan "Spike" Dinsmore, and their children Leora (Bonnie's age) and Erik. There was a bad storm the first night we were there, which soaked our trailer and everything in it. We had to let everything dry out before we drove on, but Unita had a place for all of us to sleep, and we had a great time with them, because the whole Dinsmore family loved playing games and having fun. We didn't want to leave.

In Calgary we took in the Stampede, a gift from my cousin Mary, who was living in Edmonton. Mary and her friend, Helen, took us to our first smorgasbord, in Edmonton. Wow, that was really something! We had never even heard of a smorgasbord before. Helen kept urging Doug to get more food, and she didn't have to twist his arm.

Prices in the 1970's were a lot different than now. For a campsite, the lowest we paid was $2.50 a night; the highest was $4. If a campsite we stopped at cost more than $4, we drove on until we found one that wanted less money.

When we got to B.C., we looked up a good friend from my school days, Rita Crompton; she had moved there and now lived in Langley with her husband Charlie and their son, Chuckie (who was the same age as Doug). Rita and I hadn't seen each other since we were teenagers, back in Saskatchewan. Since that time, she had been stricken with polio, which paralyzed both of her legs—a condition that her doctors said would be permanent. Somehow, while hospitalized, Rita had met Charlie, who became a good friend, and with his encouragement she managed to do better than the doctors' predictions for her recovery, although she did have to give in to the use of a wheelchair. When released from hospital, Rita married Charlie, and he did everything possible to make life good for her, including adapting a car so she could learn to drive without the use of her legs. On this trip so many years later, it was wonderful to see Rita again, and to meet her husband and son. The kids and I left our trailer parked there while we took the ferry over for a quick look at Vancouver Island.

Out west, I found the word "mountain" a bit intimidating. In northern Ontario, in the early days of the trip, the grades around Lake Superior had been steep enough for me; looking ahead on the map to see the Crow's Nest Pass, right ahead of us on Highway 3, was scary. It was always encouraging to see a tap (where you could get water for the radiator) on every steep grade—and we made use of them all!

My uncle Godford and Aunt Martina (my mother's brother married to my father's sister), who lived in Divide, Saskatchewan, had passed away but left lots of cousins to visit. By the time we got through Saskatchewan, visiting all these cousins (too numerous to name), my "young ones" were ready to head home. There is one cousin, however, that I'd like to comment on. Cousin Louis was a bachelor, but even though he was the only chef and entertainer, we had a good time with him. One particular memory stands out in my mind—a drive we took across the prairie. The land was so flat you could see, far off in the U.S.A., the low range of the Bears Paw Mountains, in Montana. I sat up front in the cab of the truck, the three kids were in the back. The purpose of the drive was to view the countryside, but Louis also wanted to give Doug a chance to shoot some rabbits, so whenever he saw a rabbit, he would stop the truck and Doug would take aim. The rabbits, however, were quite safe, because Pauline (who didn't have the heart to watch a dear little rabbit get shot) stood close enough to Doug to nudge his arm ever so slightly just as he was about to pull the trigger. Doug missed every time. The last rabbit was large, and was still sitting there after Doug missed, so cousin Louis, being quite annoyed, stopped the truck, got out, took the gun and shot the animal. He would use the meat to feed his cats and his dog. Louis and Doug weren't happy about the rabbits that were missed, but we tender hearted females were pleased.

After our visit with cousin Louis, we set our course for Ontario, glad to be heading home. Hugh was just as glad to see us when we arrived.

The East Coast…
The next year, the girls and I went to the East Coast. We were away for three weeks. We drove through the U.S. while on our way east, spending one night in beautiful Lake Placid. Another campsite that stands out in my mind was one on a cliff at Peggy's Cove. It had a firepit, and we always wanted to have a fire when we camped, so we made good use of it.

A doctor and his family camped beside us in a big RV, but they didn't have a firepit. They asked if they could join us and enjoy our fire, which was fine with us. They had collected a lot of starfish, which had to be heated to kill whatever was alive in them. We enjoyed their company, especially when the doctor found out that Pauline was in training to become an RN. While the starfish were being heated the doctor gave her some words of wisdom.

Before we parted, they gave us some of the starfish, which we put in a compartment on the outside of the trailer. It took only one day (the weather was quite warm) till we saw a lot of flies around the side of the trailer. The starfish soon got pitched out. It's hard to say whether the doctor and his family knew what they were doing, or if they just didn't cook them long enough.

While in P.E.I., we wanted to see the play Anne of Green Gables, but the play they were showing was Johnny Belinda, which was very good.

We missed having Doug along to organize the raising of the tent trailer. It was a home-made one, and a little complicated, and Doug had taken over that job on our trip out West. We managed okay, though, with just one not-so-nice experience—when we had to set it up in the rain.

End of a Chapter...
Hugh and I had twenty-five years together, with its ups and downs. I thank God that it is the good times that come to mind. Hugh was generous and outgoing. He had a great sense of humour; he could be very funny and have us all laughing. The three children God gave us were such a blessing—Pauline was born in 1952, Bonnie in 1954, and Doug in 1955. They were good "kids," a credit to Hugh and myself; they made us proud. I enjoyed being a mother. I've always thought it special that God gave women a role in His plan of creation.

CHAPTER 3

My Life with Romeo Begins

In 1974, Romeo had been sent to Pickering Nuclear Power Station to work, from the Bruce Power Station on Lake Huron. I was working as a nanny in Toronto for Dr. Paul and Carole Lerner, whose son Brett was just starting school. Brett didn't like me taking his mother's place, but we soon became good friends.

On 16 May, 1975, on a beautiful sunny day, Romeo and I were married in the City Hall. Our guests were Anne Marie (Romeo's daughter) and David Galvin (her husband, whom she had married in April), and John (Romeo's son) and Bonnie (my daughter). John and Bonnie were our witnesses. We had a fun time at the "Town and Country" Buffet. When we were informed the buffet was soon to lose, all made good use of that information—plates were well loaded. Buffet was soon to close.

Romeo had a great trip organized! We flew to Victoria that afternoon, then spent two weeks working our way back to Oshawa. We spent time sightseeing in beautiful Victoria, the Buchard Gardens being the biggest attraction; in Vancouver, we visited the Queen Elizabeth Gardens. In Vancouver, we rented a car—a red sports Camaro. Our drive through the beautiful Rocky Mountains and the time we spent in picturesque Banff was delightful. While in Banff, we drove to Pincher Creek and visited my cousin Isabel and Alf Cote, on their farm in the foothills—which was another interesting drive through mountains. We were sorry when we had to drop off the red Camaro, a week later, in Calgary, but Romeo chose the train to travel from Calgary back to Toronto, making the trip very pleasant and unforgettable.

Romeo Gets "Pushed Up the Ladder…"

Even in his early years, Romeo had been eager to learn. His ambition had always been to become an engineer, but his father didn't think an education was necessary, so he had no chance to pursue his dream. Always concerned about his lack of education, he felt he wouldn't be capable of doing the work required whenever he received a job promotion. He said many times that he had been "pushed up the ladder." Nevertheless, Romeo educated himself to the extent where he could do the work of an engineer.

Romeo was General Foreman for the carpenters, but he was also coordinator for all the trades—pipefitters, electricians, and labourers. Romeo was very interested in the job, watching always how the job was progressing, timewise etc., and determining what area needed working on first, and by which trade. For example, if two trades needed to use the crane, Romeo decided which trade would get it first, according to how the job was progressing. Such scheduling decisions were his responsibility, along with many other duties.

Romeo worked for two years at the Pickering Power Plant, and for five years in Darlington, while we were living in Oshawa. He had been sent to the Darlington site to start the plant. Quite a job and responsibility, but Romeo had worked for Hydro long enough that they knew he was capable of the task. When it came time to vote for an Assistant Structure Superintendent for the Darlington plant Romeo was told, "We expect you to apply for the job." Romeo applied and got the job.

His wisdom and his interest in his job was well recognized, and he was often asked for his opinion. On one occasion, when the cost of a project was getting out of control, Romeo was asked to sit in on a meeting with the office staff, who were trying to find ways to bring the cost down. Much thought was given to the matter, and when they didn't come up with anything productive, they asked Romeo if he had any suggestions. Romeo already had an idea in his mind; he suggested that they should cut off the night shift. He was asked, could the job still be done on time, even without the night shift? Romeo said yes, it would be. He explained that, on many occasions, he had come to work on the day shift only to find that the night shift had made a mistake which would take time to rectify, and this was leading to many lost hours. Romeo's advice was taken. The cost came down, and, timewise, the job was still on schedule. Head office would later use the improvement as an example of efficiency, and it was included in courses given to train Hydro workers. David Galvin was one man to hear of this improvement, while taking a course, and he was pretty proud that the solution had been given by his father-in-law.

Travels with the Tent Trailer...
Romeo had bought a condominium in Oshawa, where we lived for seven years. We planned on enjoying life, so that summer we bought a tent-trailer. We were told we would soon want to upgrade and trade for something larger and more convenient, but we never did; we enjoyed our little trailer with just two beds, no stove or table, etc. Romeo made two wooden boxes that were useful for storing food, dishes, pots, pans, etc. We liked a bonfire, both to look at and cook over, so these boxes were also used, when we had visitors, to sit on by the fire.

We made good use of the trailer, taking trips to the east and west coasts of Canada, to Florida, and for weekends camping around our area. East of Barrie, there were many beautiful campgrounds. My daughter Bonnie McCulloch was going to Georgian College, and later she worked in Barrie. We would let her know where we were camping, and she would often join us. At night we would listen to the wind in the tall pine trees and enjoy the scents of the forest. Lots of frogs would be croaking in a tenor tone, then the big bull frog would croak, bringing in the bass. It was quite amusing. It sounded like they were singing us to sleep.

On a trip to Florida, we took the highway that follows the top of the Blue Ridge Mountains; the descent was long, a real test for the brakes. It was a picturesque drive, with inviting campsites and hiking trails, which we were eager to enjoy.

We loved to explore, and we often took long hikes, as we always wondered what was over the next hill or around the next bend in the trail. We were never disappointed. Romeo and I liked observing nature, but he would notice a lot of things I would miss. He didn't just glance at a flower; he often looked closely, into the center, to study all the small, intricate parts.

Observing other campers while you sit around your campfire (minding your own business!) is another interesting thing to do while camping. Such was the case, one day, when Romeo had a good fire going. We noticed a young couple, staying in the site next to us, who were having difficulties making a bonfire. A little later, as we sat there enjoying our fire, we heard a voice from the darkness: "Can we enjoy your fire, too?" It was the young couple. Romeo got one of the boxes from the trailer for them to sit on, and we had a great visit. They were travelling south, with bikes on their car, which they used when they were visiting cities where they didn't want to drive. Romeo always liked talking with younger people. I think he found their new ideas refreshing; they help to keep us young, or, at least, it helps us to think that they do.

Romeo hard at work clearing the land at the Cove, pulling tree roots with the "come-along."

Jackson's Cove

Romeo was very ambitious, and always looking ahead. So, in 1976, wanting a challenge, he decided we should buy a lot and build a house for retirement. On the Thanksgiving weekend, the weather was beautiful, and the fall colours were at their peak, so we decided to go for a drive. We would go to North Bay to visit Bruce and Pauline, then we'd drive along Georgian Bay and look for a lot. Romeo had always lived near water, so by the bay would be a good place to look.

The drive to North Bay was beautiful. We stayed with Bruce and Pauline, whose twins—Julie and Sonja—were almost two years old, and very cute. I jokingly said, "Let's take them home with us, Romeo." Much to my surprise, Bruce took me up on my suggestion! They were coming to visit us in Oshawa that Sunday, for a couple of days, and would pick the twins up then. (I don't think Pauline was too keen on the idea—how could she do without them for two days?) So, our plan of looking for a lot was cancelled, the twins were buckled into their car-seats, and we were on our way. Romeo adored the children and was watching them in the rear-view mirror. We hadn't gone far when he said, "They look so lonesome and sad. Let's bring them in the front with us." We stopped and brought them in the front, where one sat on my knee, and the other between us. The next two days of their stay with us went well. We enjoyed their company, and they seemed quite happy while waiting for their parents to come for them.

The next weekend, we continued our search for a lot, inviting my sister Margaret and her husband, John McComb, to come with us. They were good company, and we would ask them their thoughts on the lots we looked at. We followed the Georgian Bay shoreline from Owen Sound to Wiarton, but the lots that were for sale didn't appeal to any of us. In Wiarton, Romeo went to the real-estate office to find out what was available in shoreline lots. The agent said one lot had just come up for sale, but it probably wasn't suitable, as the road to the site wasn't open in the winter. "We'd like to see it," said Romeo.

In this instance we didn't need Margaret's or John's opinion. As soon as Romeo saw the lot, he knew it was what he wanted, and hoped it would be what I liked. To me, it was everything one could wish for, and I was wishing Romeo might be feeling the same. We bought the lot—which was located on Hope Bay, on the west side of Georgian Bay—no hesitation. Our lot cost $20,000, which was a fair price for those days, but similar lots are now selling for $145,000.

Building Our Retirement Home…
Jackson's Cove was named for its original owner, a man named Jackson. In the early '70's, Alton and Elaine Hunter bought and developed this parcel of land—about 100 acres in size, one side of which ran along the lakefront. They paid $100,000 for the property, which was a lot of money in those days, but it paid off though, because, as I've mentioned, lots now sell for $145,000.

The house-building project was a lot of fun. Romeo and I liked working together, and we both liked being near the lake. Whether it was calm or rough, we enjoyed looking at the water or going for a swim when we wanted to cool off. It was sunny a lot of the time, but Romeo's attitude was that "the sun always shines at the Cove." (I think it was his habit to "count the sunny hours and forget the rainy days.")

Before we could start building the house, we first had to clear some trees off the lot. Anne Marie and David helped with that job. My daughter Bonnie got in on some of it too before she moved to Calgary. Bonnie said she was sorry she had to go to Calgary, as she would miss out on the fun. The trees were cut and limbed, and the branches were burned. David enjoyed the job of burning the branches, and we had some good fires. It's a wonder we didn't set the cove on fire. A few years later and it wouldn't have been allowed. After the trees were removed something had to be done with the stumps and the roots. Romeo borrowed a "come-along" from Hydro and was able to pull them out himself.

Alton Hunter made a driveway, put in the septic system, and dug the basement. We did the block work for the basement. Anne Marie and David helped us with the work: Anne Marie and I mixed mortar in the wheelbarrow while Romeo and David laid the blocks. With their help we were able to do the work by ourselves, all but the plumbing and electrical work.

Some jobs were tricky for just the two of us, but Romeo always found a way. For instance, putting the Gyproc on the cathedral ceilings. Romeo made a scaffold, the top being the same angle as the ceiling and just high enough that I could hold one end of the Gyproc up with my head and hands. Romeo had a clip to hold the other end while he nailed it. Once, he dropped the hammer, and it started sliding down the scaffold—straight for the big picture-window. All we could do was watch and hold our breath. Much to our relief it stopped in time.

It was challenging for me working on the roof until I got used to the height. It was quite warm working up there, but it was only a few steps to the water; after a dip our wet clothes would keep us cool for a while, and then we'd need another dip. Sometimes we would take a break, sit down and enjoy the gorgeous view from the roof, looking out over the lake to the Cape Croker First Nations Reserve on the far side of the lake. The location of the house was perfect, the water being only fifty feet away, with a flat rock shoreline. Behind us was the Niagara escarpment, beautiful with shades of green from the forest of trees, and the rocks and

Romeo and Mary add cedar siding to the house at the Cove. The work had progressed far enough that by October of 1982 they were able to move in to the building to complete the interior.

boulders covered with a mat of moss and a sprinkle of flowers. It took us five years to build our dream home, and we loved every hour we spent on it. Romeo didn't take any time off work; we worked on weekends and on Romeo's holidays. He took pride in the fact that we never worked on Sundays, and that there was never any alcohol consumed while the house was being built (or during all the years we lived there.) We finished a year after Romeo's last promotion. Romeo didn't want to take a reduced pension, so he decided to work another year or so. However, our new home on beautiful Hope Bay in Jackson's Cove was beckoning him. We had a talk—"how much does it cost us to live or how much is it worth to enjoy retirement now, compared to working longer to make more money so we could live 'higher on the hog?'" Romeo went to Personnel and asked how much his pension would be if he took early retirement. I'm not sure what he was told, but Romeo's comment was "I'm leaving even if I have to live on baloney!" Romeo retired in November 1982. We were never sorry. We ate baloney and anything else we desired. We enjoyed trips etc.—life to the fullest. We spent nineteen years in our home by the bay (that we thought was the best)!

In Romeo's opinion, it was always sunny at the Cove. In this photo he enjoys the sunshine, along with the beautiful view over Georgian Bay, while working on the roof of the house.

Top: *The house at the Cove in winter.*

Below: *When Ron and Jeannette Faw visited us at the Cove, Romeo used his large yellow sleigh to give Ron a ride down the hill.*

The road to the house at the Cove ran down a long, steep hill. Above: Here it is in summer and (below) in winter.

Retirement

I'm sure there has never been anyone more pleased with retirement than Romeo was. As much as he enjoyed his 33 years with Ontario Hydro, he enjoyed life after he quit just as much—maybe more. So he never regretted an early retirement.

Building the Workshop...
After the excitement and work of moving to the Cove, we had planned to just relax, enjoying the winter in our cozy house by the lake, and that beautiful fireplace that Romeo had made. We had moved in by November, and by January Romeo was getting more than a little bored. He had had enough of idle time, just his brain working (and overtime, at that). Romeo's vision of retirement had included a workshop where he would do some sort of woodwork.

Now the workshop was on his mind—how large to make it, how many tools he would need, what kind and where he would purchase

L: Romeo stands on a beam while dismantling an old barn. The salvaged material was used for the construction of a workshop at the Cove.
R: Romeo's workshop was always clean and well organized.

them. He already had the material needed for the building. As I've said, Romeo enjoyed a challenge. He could have worked another year to pay for the material for the shop, but it was a challenge to tear down a barn and use the salvaged material to build his shop. The barn had been given to us before Romeo's retirement by Mr. Le Brie from Oshawa. He was a lawyer by trade but a farmer at heart. He had an extra barn he didn't need and offered it to Romeo. It was free under one condition—that Romeo had to take it all, leaving the area where it sat clear of everything. Romeo was up for the challenge even though it was a large barn. We were fortunate not to have the clean-up job when we were done. Someone wanted the foundation for the rocks that were in it, and we were glad to give it to them, plus the task of leaving the area as if there had never been a barn. Most people would think we were "minus a brick," but we enjoyed taking the barn down; we could imagine the "barn-raising bee" that took place as it was all being put together. No nails had been used in its construction. It was interesting to see how the huge beams were joined with dovetailed joints and handmade wooden pegs.

We used our little Toyota pickup and rented a large U-Haul truck to transport the material to the Cove. Even though the U-Haul was full

The entrance to the workshop Romeo built at the Cove.

of gas when Romeo started, he had to fill it again about halfway. Before we got to the end of our trip it was showing empty again. It was after midnight by now, and there were no nearby gas stations, so we had to leave the U-Haul on the side of the road while we continued on to the Cove, which was only a short distance away. The next morning, we went to Lion's Head, a little village about twenty minutes away, to get some gas. There always seems to be some older retired men wherever there is something going on, just sitting and relaxing, putting in time, minding their own business, but hearing all that's being said. Such was the case this day. One of them said to Romeo, "I think you have another gas tank that is probably full in the U-Haul. The switch to turn it on is on the left-hand side of the driver's seat." Romeo found out he was right—there was probably enough gas for the full trip, if Romeo had used both tanks.

Concerning the workshop, Romeo couldn't put up with just thinking about it, there had to be some action. Much to my sorrow, because, regardless of the cold weather, the lumber covered with snow and ice,

Romeo's workshop was equipped with all the tools he needed, such as this planer, which was used for smoothing the surfaces of the lumber he used for his projects.

the shop was going to be built—and now. It was fine to go skiing in the cold, but to work with wood covered in snow and ice didn't appeal to me. However, making the foundation was a job for more than one person, so I was Romeo's help. We joked about the let-down this must have been for Romeo. When Romeo worked for Hydro, he had lots of men; all he had to do was tell the men what had to be done and it was done. Now he only had one worker to give orders to, and that one was a woman, and one not in the habit of taking orders. But, regardless of the weather (and the lone female helper) we enjoyed the job, and by spring the shop was finished and ready for the tools.

The shop had a loft, where Romeo piled his lumber. He also made a kiln in the loft, for drying the wood. There was a picture-window that once belonged to the Lion's Head Missionary church. While Romeo was helping the church with some renovations, it had been decided that the window wouldn't be needed anymore. So, what to do with the window? Claren Martin, the minister, said, "Give it to somebody deserving of it. Give it to Romeo." So Romeo's shop had a beautiful picture window facing the lake.

There was enough tin from the salvaged barn to cover the roof and walls of the shop. We painted the walls reddish brown. Some of the big timbers were used for the mantle and hearth of the beautiful brick fireplace Romeo made in our house. Now more timbers were used for the shop floor. Romeo cut the timbers into one-foot lengths, stood them on end, and sank them into the soil. They made a good solid floor. Grandchildren Bonnie and David were pretty young then, but they carried fine stones from the shore to fill any cracks.

Romeo loved his workshop, and he spent many happy hours there. Much thought had been put into its construction, and when he finished, it was exactly what he wanted. Sometimes in the winter I'd go out with my knitting to sit and watch Romeo work. The shop had an airtight stove which kept it warm, and on cold winter days, with the view of the snow through the window, and the sight of the blazing fire behind the glass in the door of the stove, it would be quite cozy. They were special times.

Top: The workshop was a cozy place. Even in winter Romeo could enjoy working on his many projects.

Below: Romeo works on house renovations for my sister Margaret.

By the Work of His Hands

Romeo's Work Projects…
At first, Romeo made small things like doll furniture, small tables and chairs for children. We had friends in Lion's Head, Doug and Marlene Hill, and one day Marlene told Romeo she wanted him to make her a china cabinet. Romeo said he wasn't capable of that, but Marlene insisted he could do it. They went to some furniture stores in Owen Sound to look at china cabinets, and Marlene soon had him convinced. As well as looking at furniture, Romeo bought the blueprints for a china cabinet. The cabinet he built was beautiful, and that was the start of him building large furniture.

To build large furniture you need the ability to read blueprints. Now, remember, Romeo had little education—possibly Grade 6, and that was in French, yet he knew how to read such plans. This came about because while working for Hydro in northern Ontario in winter (which wasn't pleasant—so very cold, especially on the hands), Romeo had noticed that the men wearing white hats were mostly inside, where it was warmer. Romeo asked one day, "How do you get to wear a white hat?" He was told, "You have to be a foreman." To become a foreman Romeo knew he would have to learn how to read blueprints, so he retrieved them from waste baskets and studied them, until he knew what each stroke meant.

Romeo gave Marlene credit for his beginning of making furniture. She said he could, and he did. From then on nothing was impossible; Romeo made anything people asked for. This took in a large range of items: any kind of furniture; kitchen cabinets; canoes; even a rack made to hold a stretcher, mounted on skis. This rack was made to be pulled behind a snowmobile to rescue sick people or accident victims from places where other vehicles couldn't go. There was space on the end of the skis for someone to stand and steady the stretcher. This was an order from Wiarton Paramedic, Greg Vermilyea. I often thought of our hill, which leads down from the escarpment, and hoped that I would never have to use that means of transportation.

Top: *"How do you get to wear a white hat?"* Romeo asked in his early days with Ontario Hydro.

Right: One of the safety awards Romeo received for 20 years of no lost work time for his men due to accidents on the job.

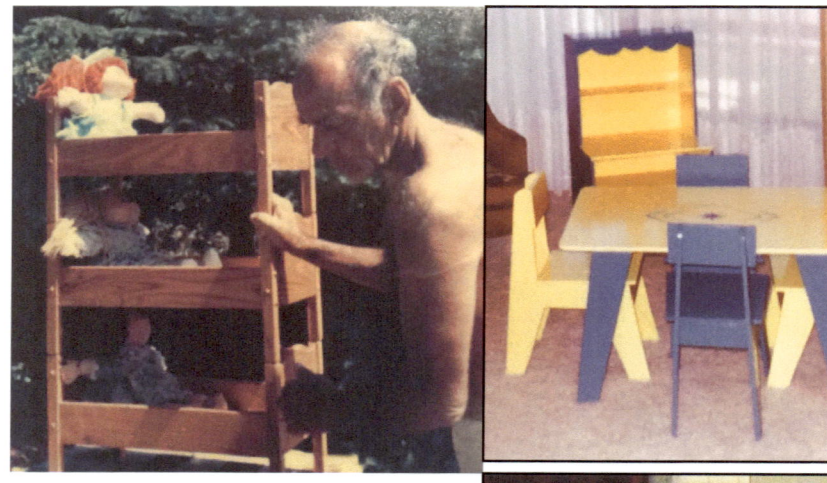

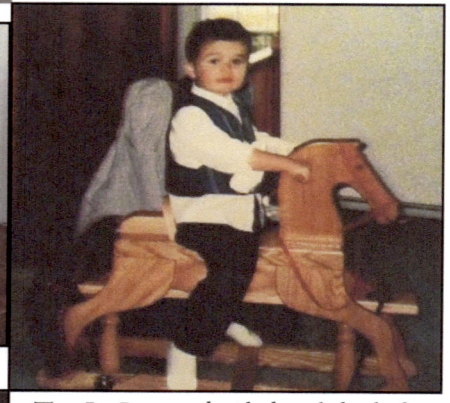

Top L: Romeo built bunk beds for three lucky Cabbage Patch dolls.

Top R: This table set has been enjoyed by two generations of kids.

Middle: Ride 'em, cowboy! Gary Russell (left) and Jordan Bouchard ride the rocking-horses made by Romeo (aka Pére).

L: Jonathan Clark (the first of my great-grandchildren) relaxes in a platform-style rocking-chair made by Pére.

Top: Seven children's rocking-chairs in production in Romeo's workshop. A trip to the Cove was not complete without a visit to the workshop to see Romeo's latest projects.

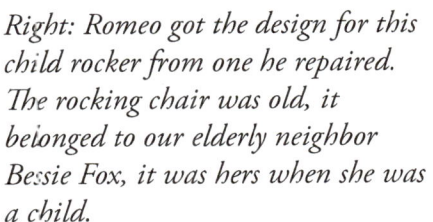

Right: Romeo got the design for this child rocker from one he repaired. The rocking chair was old, it belonged to our elderly neighbor Bessie Fox, it was hers when she was a child.

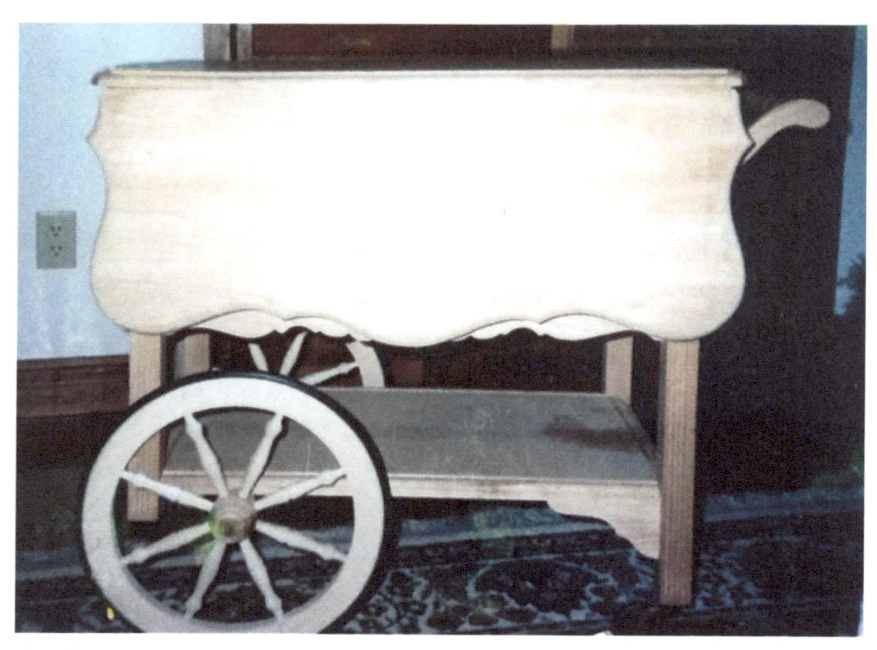

Other furniture projects undertaken by Romeo: Top: A drop-leaf tea-wagon. Below: A roll-top desk.

Work for the Church / Family Projects / Volunteer Work...

Along with all the work Romeo did in his shop, he also did home repairs and building renovations. Romeo did volunteer work for churches, sometimes charging for material used. The churches were: Missionary Church, Lion's Head; Presbyterian Church, Dornoch; and a Catholic church in Wiarton.

Romeo did some work for his brother, Florient, in Quebec City. Florient and his wife stayed in their cottage, and Romeo and I lived in their house while working there. In his workshop, Romeo cut up all the material he would need to make kitchen cupboards for Florient's home. Being just boards, we managed to put all the pieces into our Nissan Pathfinder, and Romeo put it all together when we got to the house in Quebec City. He put the finish on the cupboards after they were put together and in place. He made clothes closets more accessible by taking off the doors, making the opening larger, and putting on two folding doors. He also made a closet under the stairway into a place for a washer and dryer.

Romeo fixed the plumbing; the water from the dishwasher was going into the bathtub before draining out. Since they lived on the second floor and the pipes were old, rusty and corroded, he had to rent some pipe wrenches to get the pipes apart. It wasn't an easy job, but when Romeo finished, all worked well, from the top (second floor) to the basement and out. I did some painting and some wallpapering.

We enjoyed our time in Quebec City. We visited Old Quebec City, more than once. Also visited Liette, Florient's ex-wife, who we were both fond of.

Romeo did a major job for my sister Margaret and her husband John. He started by making the living/dining room larger. To do that, the roof had to be extended a possible six feet, so the wall would be even with the wall of the rest of the house. Being an old house, this made more work than "meets the eye." When finished, he had worked on the family room and wood room area. A new floor had to be put under the family and wood rooms. Roger and Greg (Marg and John's son and son-in-law) did the digging that had to be done under the floor. John, Margaret and I were there to help when needed. Margaret is a great cook and we were well fed. I have a picture of Margaret in her work coveralls, making a pie. We had fun then and were with Margaret and John when Romeo did some work on Roger's house and their other son's (Wayne) cottage.

Pam (Margaret's daughter), and her husband Greg Vermilyea came for a visit, and to "pick Romeo's brain." They were doing some repairs on a house they bought. Romeo is always interested and ready to give advice. In this case, the advice needed was how to raise the floor. Romeo ended up helping with the project.

After the floor was jacked up there were lots of cracks in the walls, especially the upper floor. The three bedrooms had to be gutted and walls redone. Romeo headed the team and the four of us went to work. We really enjoyed our time with Pam and Greg, got to really know them, and Pam made delicious lunches. There was some work on the main floor, and Romeo also made beautiful kitchen cupboards for Pam. Years later, Pam was sad at having to leave the cupboards behind, when they moved to a larger house.

Romeo wanted to help my son Doug and his wife Marianne (beekeepers in Alberta) build a platform by their honey house, strong enough to hold the barrels of honey. It would be a big job, Doug thought, and costly. Instead of digging below the frostline to make a firm foundation, Romeo suggested they construct a floating foundation, like the one he would help to build later, for the duplex building in Haiti, where the wet and dry seasons work the ground like the frost does the soil in Canada. It didn't take long to do the job, and the project cost a lot less than Doug thought it would.

When Doug and Marianne (his fantastic teammate) started their honey business, the property they bought had a barn on it, which had been used to stable horses. They turned the stable into a honey house. As the business progressed more space was needed, and the honey house expanded along with the business. Romeo liked to be there when work like that needed to be done, but he didn't think much of going to the bee-yards with Doug. Once, when Doug took the lid off a box, the bees came swarming out, and they were in a foul mood. Romeo took off running, but some of the bees followed him. Doug shouted after Romeo, "Turn and run between the trees!" Romeo did as he was told, and since bees always fly in a straight line (hence the term "bee-line"), they just kept going. Romeo was relieved. He was on for all kinds of jobs, but if it had to do with bees, you could count him out.

Romeo never liked to be idle very long. When visiting, my "kids" always seemed to have a job for him. Once, at Bonnie and Peter's home in Calgary, he cut and finished an opening in a wall, making a shortcut from their kitchen to the dining-room. It was Bonnie who wanted the opening made, and she was sure Romeo could do the job, but Peter was skeptical about it, so Bonnie had Romeo cut the opening while Peter was away at work. Peter was surprised (and very pleased) at the result; he said it added to the value of the house.

When the Bruce Clark family moved to Thunder Bay, Pauline and the girls drove up with me. We had a nice trip, taking most of three days. David came with his dad. Bruce wanted Romeo to come and paid his air fare. So, Romeo came after work on Friday, and by Saturday night he had made a study for Bruce in the basement of the townhouse they were moving into.

About the office and how it got put together so fast… When Romeo knows there is a job to be done his brain starts working overtime. The moving van was supposed to be in Thunder Bay by early afternoon, but it had motor problems (it didn't arrive till the next day), so there was no furniture, no beds, etc.

The Clarks had friends who asked us all to join them for supper and offered us a place to stay for the night. That was fine for the Clarks, but Romeo had the job on his mind; he said we would go out for something to eat, and sleep in the townhouse, on the trailer mattress we had in the back of our truck. As soon as everyone left, we went out for "fast food" to eat, and then to get material for the office. Romeo had already figured out what he needed. He worked late into the night to have a good start on the office, so he was sure he could finish the job the next day. Bruce was pleased with Romeo's work, and thought it well worth the air fare.

This is the first piece of furniture Romeo made, thanks to the support of Marlene Hill, who was confident he was capable of building such large-scale projects.

Romeo's niece Thérèse designed this floor to ceiling china cabinet and was thrilled with Romeo's work, including table and Windsor-back chairs.

This furniture, double cabinet, rocking chair and stool Romeo made for his nephew Rosaire Cardinal and wife Jacqueline. The little stool was made from the pattern of a milking stool. It was very popular and Romeo made lots of these.

Above: This dining room set was made for my sister Margaret & husband John McComb. The dining room is the extension that Romeo built on to their house.

Below: Our friends from the Cove, Doug and Donna Gammie, designed and ordered this entertainment centre. The doors for the TV open and can then slide back out of sight. There are two attractive and useful cabinets on the sides.

Above Left: Romeo designed the fireplace as well as made it. Beautiful to look at on a snowy day. We don't use much electricity for heat. Romeo also made the candle holders on the mantle.

Above Right: This mirror and drawer unit was popular, they made a nice wedding gift. Romeo got lots of orders.

Below: Romeo built this cottage kitchen for his son John & daughter-in-law Maureen.

Romeo did lots of jobs for the people living in the apartments above the Golden Dawn Nursing Home in Lion's Head. He would make some improvements in one apartment, then there would be a few more residents wanting the same thing done. One woman wanted a small dining-room suite made. Romeo made a small table, only four chairs, and a curio cabinet. Two other ladies ordered the same. They weren't from the Golden Dawn but lived in small apartments. Romeo liked working there. The elderly people were so appreciative, they all liked Romeo.

Hydroponic Garden…

Even though Romeo had lots of work in his shop—there were always orders to be filled—he still wanted to do something else. He had told me of having gardens, in his former years, and the success and enjoyment he experienced from gardening. It was not just a hobby; these had been large gardens, producing lots of vegetables for the family.

We didn't have enough space for a garden at the Cove, plus the soil wasn't suitable (too much rock and not enough soil), but Romeo came up with the idea of starting a hydroponic garden. It would be a great project for the winter months, and once it was set up, it wouldn't take up too much of his shop time. The house wasn't large enough for a hydroponic garden, so Romeo decided to add another room, ten feet by twelve feet. He had someone put in the foundation; then he built the rest of the building. There was a large picture window, and Romeo planned on putting the garden—a plastic enclosure—in front of it, so the plants would have lots of light.

Romeo didn't believe in reading too many instructions. Why should he when he could usually figure things out for himself? He did however, at some point, get the information that you don't use natural lighting for hydroponic growing. It must all be artificial and very bright and included the use of a heat lamp. By this time Romeo had already cut and finished an opening in the wall, connecting the new room with the living room, so the garden could take advantage of the natural light. Now that he had to move the garden because of the revised light requirements, the opening was in the wrong spot: not only would the finished opening have to be closed, a new one would have to be made at the other end of the wall, by the window.

Another one of Romeo's good traits was, no matter how big or small the mistake he had to rectify, he never got upset. It was a case of, "It has to be done, so do it, no complaining." The completed hydroponic garden consisted of a plastic enclosure, four feet by six feet, with just enough room for someone to move around while tending the plants inside. Romeo was pleased; when he finished, it was exactly what he needed, and he produced lots of beautiful tomatoes and English cucumbers.

The care and watering of the hydroponic system took very little time each day, but it couldn't be left for more than two days without that attention. If we wanted to go away for any length of time Romeo would have to do away with all the plants and start over again when we got back home. For that reason, Romeo only used it for a few years. That was okay, because he enjoyed the experience, and when the enclosure was demolished, we had an extra room, which we set up as a family room, with a television, etc. Romeo especially enjoyed this room, and I think he thought of it as mostly his room. He used it for an escape when company came that he wasn't involved with, or when he just wanted a quiet place to sit and read.

Life at the Cove

We lived below the Niagara escarpment, and because the hill was steep, the road was closed in the winter; cars were left in a parking lot at the top of the hill. You either walked up the hill or used a snowmobile. We didn't walk up the hill for long. Troy Hunter, Alton and Elaine's son, who lived at the top of the hill, had a snowmobile. He was 16 and wanted to buy a car, so he sold the snowmobile to Romeo. We had an old Toyota car, in bad shape, which we sold to Troy for $200. He took the car to school, where it was used as a project for the mechanical class to work on, and they did a good job repairing it. Troy had it painted yellow, and named it Bumble Bee. The first time he took Bumble Bee out for a drive, an elderly man made a quick turn in front of Troy, who couldn't stop quickly enough. The car was a write-off, though the motor was still running. It was hard for Troy to turn it off, as he knew it would never run again.

Above: Romeo's nephew, Christian Heroux from Montreal, was very excited and pleased with the armoire! There was also a harvest table and six chairs in the order.

It was a winter wonderland when the snow came, and we had a lot of fun. Since the road wasn't open in the winter, it was only our tracks on foot or on skis, later our snowmobiles, to disturb the snow. With no traffic on the hill, it was perfect for tobogganing, which was enjoyed by many people, both young and old—our kids and grandkids (we moved away from the Cove before our great-grandchildren could join in the fun), as well as our friends from Lion's Head. I, too, couldn't resist, and would take my turn on the toboggan. After a long ride down on the toboggan, someone (usually Romeo, when he decided to join the fun) would go down on the snowmobile to pull the toboggan—and everyone on it—back up the hill. Most toboggans have room for three riders, but it was extra fun when the Hill family came, because their toboggan could hold six people if they squeezed themselves together.

We had two snowmobiles, which gave us lots of enjoyment on the trails, as well as transportation. Romeo would use the snowmobile and sleigh to take furniture from his shop to customers waiting on top of the hill. Our minister, Charles Gingrich, wanted Romeo to make a footboard to match the headboard for his bed. Charles brought the headboard and Romeo met him at the top of the hill with the snowmobile and sleigh. The minister was being very protective of the headboard, so he held it while he sat at the edge of the sleigh. Unfortunately, he sat on the wrong side of the sleigh. As Romeo rounded the corner at the bottom of the hill Charles' weight tipped the sleigh over. When Romeo looked back to see if all was okay, there was the minister, lying on his back, the headboard on top of him.

Some people just walked the hill, some people needed a ride. Such was the case with our friends the Dixons. Doreen was good to walk, but Bob's health was failing, and Doreen asked me if I would give him a ride up the hill. As Bob took a seat on the back of the snowmobile, I told him, "Bob, you have to hold on to me." He didn't. When we turned the corner to go up the hill I said again, "Bob, you have to hold on to me." The hill was full of big bumps, and if you didn't keep up your speed you were apt to get stuck in between. It wasn't a smooth ride, and by the time we got to the top Bob was really holding on. Doreen, already at the top, said to her husband, "Now, Bob, thank Mary." With that, Bob replied, "And thank God!"

Another source of enjoyment at the Cove was the Bruce Trail, which ran just above us. We could drive to the top and start there, or just cross the road at our house and start climbing. We walked it many times by ourselves, or with people who came to visit. One would make many stops on the way up the hill to rest or just to take in the view. The water was beautiful to look at, as well as refreshing for a cool dip, especially after a sauna. The water was very clear when we first moved to the Cove, and for a few years it was still pure enough to drink. No one had a well.

Special Visitors from the West...
The cove was a great place to live while the grandchildren were growing up. We enjoyed our grandchildren "to the max." They spent a lot of time with us, especially Pauline's children. The other ones were too far away. Ruth, Mary, and Sarah from Alberta were very special to us, but we only got to see them when we visited them out there or when the girls came east with their parents, Doug and Marianne—except for the visits each of the girls made alone to the cove when they were 15. This was very special!

When Ruth came, we took her to Niagara Falls. Ruth and I enjoyed Marineland. We did all the rides, even the terrifying rollercoaster. These rides were not for Romeo. Not that Romeo didn't want to enjoy them, like us (he was all for having fun), but the motion made him sick. It was a good trip and Ruth treated us to a spaghetti dinner(!), which was very thoughtful, for a 15-year-old.

When Mary's turn came, she spent time in Port Hope with Pauline, Bruce, and her cousins. After a few days Mary and Bonnie came to the Cove to spend time with us. Romeo always enjoyed the grandchildren. One day he packed a lunch and three of them climbed up the cliff to the Bruce Trail. They had a good hike, stopping at a picturesque spot overlooking the bay, to enjoy the good lunch Romeo had packed.

A few years later it was Sarah's turn. Sarah also had a good time in Toronto with Aunt Pauline, Uncle Bruce, and cousins. It was fun to have Sarah at the Cove. We did lots of hiking with the girls, and they all enjoyed the sauna and a dip in the cool water after. The water in Georgian Bay is always cooler than Lake Huron, and the sauna made it more enjoyable. (In the winter, after a sauna, we would go out in the snow in our bathing suits and toss snowballs at each other—not Romeo—a sauna was enough for him; or someone brave enough—like Pauline—would attempt to make snow-angels.)

We loved our home by the Bay, but we had to be realistic—we were getting old (as everyone does), and soon too old to make our way up that hill by snowmobile. Also, Anne Marie (Romeo's daughter) has MS and spends most of her time in bed. We thought that we might be of some use to her and her husband Doug, if we lived closer, so we decided to sell

When Romeo retired from his workshop, he sold his tools to Rosaire Cardinal. A smiling Rosaire pulls the dolly while Romeo and Gilles steady the load.

our house. The thought of having to leave our home by the bay was much easier to take when we had a purpose to leave. Romeo thought his shop days were over (it's hard to believe, but I think he enjoyed the fact), and he sold everything in the shop to his nephew Rosaire Cardinal, in Ville Marie.

Note: Twenty years after its construction, the property known affectionately as The Cove was put up for sale: "A sunny, southern exposure, along a 153' lakefront lot; great area for boating, fishing, hiking, and all kinds of winter activities; for seasonal or year-long living; with a drilled well; amenities include a sauna, fireplace…"

At the Cove…
If the sun dances
on the waves
that lap the rocky shore,
The wind chimes will sparkle
Sparkle and break
the silence
that lingers forever
Between the Niagara Escarpment
and the Georgian Bay
The caressing winds
And the inky nights
The cedars frame
the scene
A picture of a place
A place where my family gathers.
(by my granddaughter Mary McCulloch (now Olthuis) – age 15)

Port Elgin

The Work of His Hands…
To our way of thinking, we bought the perfect home in Port Elgin: a small white bungalow, right size for two, and large enough to squeeze family in. And we were right; we enjoyed our little house. But we had been in our new home in Port Elgin for only about two years when Romeo started missing his workshop. However, if there is a will there is always a way, and when Romeo got something in his mind, some way it materialized.

Our house has a full basement but only half of it was finished so Romeo decided to put a shop on the other side. He put up heavy plastic for walls and put insulation in any open spaces to keep all the dust inside. Romeo bought all new tools and continued where he left off, making more beautiful furniture. Even though the shop was small he still made large furniture. Two pieces were too large to take up the stairs, so Romeo had to cut a portion from the top, then glue it back in place when he got them up the stairs. He made a good job of repairing the join.

We moved to Port Elgin in 2001. Romeo worked fourteen years in the shop in the basement and retired again in 2015.

Two of Romeo's favourite stores were Lee Valley and Wellbeck Saw Mill. Long ago, possibly in the early '40's, a family named Miller started the Wellbeck Saw Mill. It's now a store situated about four miles north of the village of Durham, a few miles off Highway 6 (one might say "in the middle of nowhere"—the area for miles around is farmland). At first it was just a sawmill, but the Millers built a store beside the mill, and as the store business grew, the sawmill was used less, until they stopped sawing lumber completely. The store is huge: its merchandise consists of any kind of hardware, building material, and wood-working machines, plus all the appliances for kitchens and bathrooms.

When Mr. Miller decided the store was too much for him, he gave it to his daughter Bonnie. Bonnie, having worked in the store for years, was a natural for the job. Her husband Ralph, who also worked in the store, was a great help; he knew all there was to know about the woodworking machines, and how to pass the knowledge on. Ralph became a great friend of Romeo's, plus being a source of all the information Romeo needed.

My mother "Kate" was born in a log house a half mile from where the store is situated, close to the small village called Wellbeck. Mother said they referred to Wellbeck as "well back in the woods." The village has been gone for a long time. The area where it was is very pretty, with a river winding through the village, plus lots of trees—hardwood and evergreen trees. It is truly well back in the woods.

We spent hours in Lee Valley and in Wellbeck's. Romeo was always looking for some new tool on the market, or more ideas for using the tools he had, or a better way of working. He also looked for new challenges. One day in Lee Valley, before we moved to Port Elgin, Romeo saw a blueprint for a child's rocking chair; it looked like a challenge—it was a platform rocker with a caned seat and back. Romeo had never done any caning, so that was something to learn, but it was no problem after he found some instructions. Romeo bought the blueprint and made an adorable little chair, which sat in our living-room for many years. The grand-daughters would admire it and wondered who might be the lucky one to get it. Romeo and I decided we would give it to the grandchild who gave us our first great-grandchild.

In 1999, Sonja (our grand-daughter) married Jim Russell. In 2000, our grandson David married Marlene Haalstra. Marlene got pregnant before Sonja. Sonja made the comment, "I really wanted that rocking chair," which Romeo heard. Soon after, Romeo said to me, "I wonder how many tools I would have to buy to make more rocking chairs?" I think this is when he realized how much he missed his shop at the Cove, and so turned his thoughts to setting up a shop in the basement. Romeo didn't just make one rocker for Sonja, but seven—one for each grandchild. I got to keep the very first one he had made. I didn't want to give it up.

Romeo had orders for two more rocking chairs.

Many years later, after Romeo had retired for the last time, a great-niece, Jacklyn Cook, married and had children. Jacklyn was a favourite of Romeo's (another was niece Rainy Given), and the feeling was mutual. Jacklyn was always good to Romeo: at family gatherings she talked and joked with him: she would sit with him and make sure he got lots of food.

Jacklyn wanted so much to have a child's rocking chair made by Uncle Romeo, but it was too late for Romeo to start all over again. So, Jacklyn got the very first rocker Romeo made. I gladly gave it up. Jacklyn was pleased, and Romeo was happy to give it to her.

Romeo also made rocking-horses for three of the grandchildren and got an order for one. He made cedar chests for each of the seven grandchildren. Romeo was a caring and loving Grandpa to all my grandchildren. Pauline's twins, the oldest grandchildren, were born five months before Romeo and I were married, so they all thought of Romeo as 'Grandpa,' and thought as much of him as they did of me. This was to be expected, as Romeo gave them as much attention as I did.

Back patio at our home in Port Elgin is a lovely place to relax on a warm day.

Port Elgin received a lot of snow that year, but Romeo didn't mind the work. Below: That's our house in Port Elgin, behind an impressive wall of snow.

Top: Haiti, 1984. Says Doug Hill: "He may have been explaining how the lintel was going to be framed. He was the smartest guy on site for sure. Or, he may have been exasperated. It happens."
R: The Hill family played a significant role in Mary and Romeo's retirement activities. Doug, Marlene and children John, Emily and Lucy.
Below: Lucy and John help the Lion's Head church welcome Mary and Romeo back from Haiti in 1985

CHAPTER 4

Missions & Work Teams

Haiti (1984 twice)...
When we moved to the cove in the Lion's Head area, we attended both the Catholic and the Missionary churches. After about a year later, we heard from our friends, Marlene and Doug Hill, that they had been on a Work Team to Ecuador, through the Missionary church, and had enjoyed the experience very much. It sounded good to Romeo and me, and we asked the church to let us know when the next team would be going. This would be the first of nine mission trips Romeo and I would embark on.

In February of 1984 a team was going to Haiti, and we were on it, along with Doug. There were ten members on the team, and we helped to build a church in Port-au-Prince. (We liked the experience so much we asked when we could come back by ourselves to work. We were told that we could come whenever we wanted to. We were back in October 1984, stayed for six months, and returned home in April the following year.) Our minister, Rob Marcus, and former minister Claren Martin prayed for us—a safe time there and God's blessings. We felt blest for this opportunity and were very excited.

Before we left, the congregation gave us a bag of small gifts, wrapped, to be opened on Christmas Day. My sister Margaret made a special meal for us and all my siblings before we left. Pauline also flew from Thunder Bay to be with us for the last days, which was wonderful. It was going to be six months before I would see Pauline again. It was all very exciting. It was a tearful goodbye. We were pretty "wired up" by the time we left.

In Haiti we had a comfortable little apartment with two rooms. The kitchen had all the appliances we have at home, and there was a shower in the corner of the bedroom. The water wasn't heated for the shower but was never very cold. We shared an outhouse with two men from the radio facility room next door, plus geckos and cockroaches (which weren't welcome). Romeo's advice on the situation was to slam the door a few times before you go in, and the unwanted guests will disappear. Don't sit too long though, as they will come back. There were few flies or mosquitoes (the little geckos helped to get rid of them), and the only insect I can recall were fireflies—we would see them flashing around as we lay in bed at night. There were some malarial mosquitos, but we were never sick with malaria. As for the geckos, we soon got used to having them in our apartment.

Romeo and Mary install a metal roof on the clinic they helped build at La Jeune, Haiti.

Romeo was the good handyman they needed—he did carpentry, electric, and plumbing. He was very much appreciated for his skills, and more. On Wednesday nights we had Bible Study and Prayer Meeting, but it was also a night to "pick Romeo's brains." They soon realized he was not only knowledgeable about construction methods, but that he was an expert on solving problems, and they made good use of both abilities. His advice was used many times. They were having trouble with the roof of the clinic, which was leaking badly. The changing of the seasons—hot, dry weather followed by extremely wet weather—worked the soil, like frost. This would make the walls move, which would cause cracks in the roof. One such crack was over their medical supplies. Romeo said, "Put a tin roof over it all." Romeo and I got the job. It was hot weather, a hundred degrees or more most of the time, but because there was no humidity it wasn't too hard to take. Most people took a break from noon to two o'clock, which was the hottest time of the day. Romeo and I were happy to do the same.

Romeo also told them how to build the foundation for a duplex that would face the same problem as the clinic—hot, dry weather followed by a very wet season, which worked the ground. Romeo told them, "Don't go down deep, build a floating slab as a foundation." They took his advice, and with the help of a number of Haitian men, Romeo and I made the foundation. (We heard, years later, that they had had no problems with cracks.) When they were building the roof of the duplex, Romeo suggested that they use half as many support trusses as they had planned. In Canada, more would have been required because of the snow load, but this was Haiti. The reduction saved money.

During our six months in Haiti, we worked and lived in three different areas: The first location (and the place we called home) was La Jeune, where we stayed the longest, and did the most work—a lot of small jobs. The second was Gens de Nantes, which was close to the Dominican border, where we helped Zelda, the nurse in charge of the clinic. Finally, there was Cerca Carvajal, which was south of La Jeune.

Working with Don and Karen Danz in Cerca Carvajal, our job was to help in the building of a duplex. Don's main job in Haiti had to do with agriculture. He showed farmers how to plant and cultivate gardens, using better methods than what they were currently doing; he also taught them how to raise pigs (the main meats were chicken, goat, and beef). Don wasn't a pastor, but he would go to church where they seldom had a minister and fill in. One Sunday, Don asked Romeo and me to go with him. We drove part of the way and then walked for two hours. Since the countryside in that area was so beautiful, it was a pleasure. Most of the time we followed a cow path, with low, tree-covered mountains on either side. We crossed some shallow rivers, having to remove our shoes at times.

The church was just a frame made of poles, with palm branches attached to them to form the walls, as well as the roof; the branches were placed far enough apart so the breeze could pass through to keep it cool. Since the language was Creole, much like French, Romeo could understand a lot of what was said. My French wasn't as good, and I spent most of the time looking at the beautiful country through the spaces between the branches. There were some amusing moments... At one point, a dog chased a chicken, which flew into the dried palm branches of the roof and made quite a racket. Some of the seats were just poles to sit on, and the church was packed; with too many on a seat, a pole broke during the sermon, causing quite a commotion.

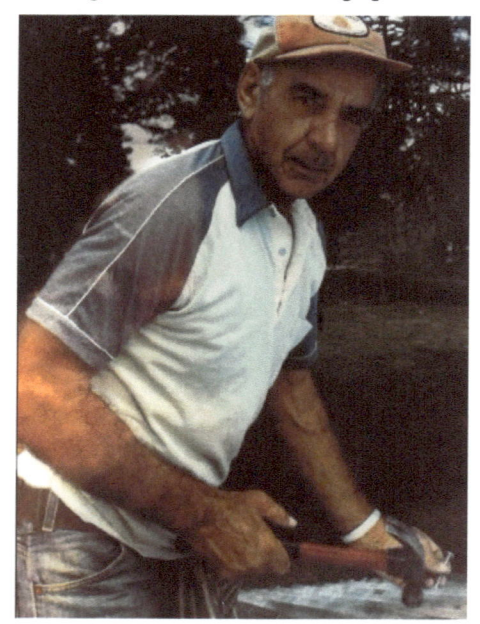

Romeo, hard at work. La Jeune, Haiti.

At Gens de Nantes we built a building to serve as a waiting room—a place to sit or stand while waiting for your turn with the doctor. The old building was made mostly of wood and the termites had done a job on it. It was about to fall down. The new building would have a cement floor, cement posts to support a thatched roof, and a surrounding wall that was three-and-a-half feet high, made of cement blocks. Cement was used because it would make the building termite-proof. A long bench was built along the walls. To get to the clinic some people would have to walk or ride (if they were fortunate enough to own a horse or donkey) over rough terrain—most of the time only a path—for hours. When they arrived, they would be grateful to find a place where they could sit down.

Along with the termites, there were also fire ants, which I became aware of while we were working on another building. I was at one end of a line we were stretching to mark the corners, and it just happened that there was a hill of fire ants in my corner. When you step on these ants you don't exactly stand still, and Romeo was getting quite annoyed because I wasn't holding the line straight or still. He wouldn't believe my excuse, said it was my imagination. A little later, when Romeo had to work in that area, he realized it wasn't imagination, because while he was trying to prove it was my imagination the ants found their way up his pant leg. Romeo had to go (run!) to the outhouse and remove his trousers to get rid of his unwanted visitors. The Haitians—who were always standing around, watching what we were doing—thought it was funny, and they really had a good laugh. Zelda also got a chuckle out of it, and Romeo was reminded of the event more times than he liked. This building was smaller than the waiting room, with enough space for four beds. It would be used by people who needed to spend more than one day at the clinic.

There were other jobs to be done at the clinic, besides construction. New cupboards were built, and some of the old cupboards needed to have doors and drawers replaced or repainted.

Zelda had a small building, a depot, where she kept her supplies. She had a lot of supplies; if patients admitted to the hospital needed drugs, she would provide them. She would canvas for items she needed (mostly medical supplies) whenever she went on furlough. As Zelda was

Top: In Haiti, going to church could involve a two-hour hike. It was always an interesting walk.

Below: A visit to an outdoor church, in Cerca Carvajal, Haiti.

very efficient, and she loved the Haitian people, she was very successful in her efforts. She would have the supplies shipped to Haiti in metal barrels, which were kept in the depot and used for storage. The depot was infested with termites and rats, and the building hadn't been cleaned for years. Zelda didn't want to ask anyone to do the job, so I volunteered. It wasn't a pleasant job. Poison had been used to control the rats, and I found more than their droppings (some of the dead rats were nothing more than skeletons), but I believe that a person can do anything, if they just make up their mind to do it. Hearing Zelda's appreciation, after the job was done, made it all worthwhile.

Romeo had great respect for Zelda. He could see how she never spared herself. Zelda was in Haiti to love and help the Haitian people as a nurse and to pass on the good news of salvation. Because of this Romeo would never refuse any work Zelda had for him. We always enjoyed our times with her. One reason was the food, which was not only different, but special.

On one occasion, it had rained the day before we were to visit her, and when it rains in Haiti, it pours—you could get over half-a-foot of rain, all at one time. Romeo was told we may as well wait a day before leaving for Zelda's, as the river between La Jeune and Cape Haitien would be too high for us to drive across. But Romeo had a job to do at Zelda's, and he wasn't about to sit around, waiting until the river went down. In Pigeon, which was halfway to the river, we were told there was traffic coming south that couldn't get through the rising water. There was a bus and a truck on the far side of the river when we got there. Romeo got me and a couple of Haitians (who were standing around wondering how smart or dumb the foreigners were) to wade across, to see if there were any deep holes, or to know for sure where the road was. The water came over my knees, which seemed okay to Romeo. He put the Bronco in high gear, stepped on the gas, and came through okay, with water gushing out on both sides of the vehicle. We were on our way once more.

There were lots of interesting things to see and do in Haiti. One thing was going to church—the getting there, and all that went on to make a Sunday Service. I will tell you of one Sunday at Zelda's.

It was Zelda's birthday and also Thanksgiving. In Haiti, any celebration is called a Fete. Zelda had asked us all to come and celebrate, so late Saturday afternoon, ten of us arrived at her home. We all brought food, and Zelda had a feast ready as well. She was very generous, and always had twice as much food as was needed. The house was full, but we all managed to get a good sleep, and were ready for an early start in the morning for church.

We left for church at 7:15 a.m., in three Broncos. These were the vehicles they used in Haiti, since they were thought to be extra powerful, which was needed for the rough roads (and sometimes no roads!). There are low mountains in that area, which made it a beautiful drive. It took an hour and a half to go part way up a mountain to pick up four Haitians. The next five miles weren't much more than a cow path, which took forty-five minutes to drive. This was supposed to be a road to take out lumber; it was made in 1952 and wasn't used much after that. After the road became impassable, we walked for the last half hour. It was a pleasant walk through lush green meadows, in some places there were lots of trees, and once we had to cross a river. We had to remove our shoes, but the day was quite warm, and the cool water felt good on our feet.

The service (maybe call it an event, because of all that went on) started at 9:45 a.m., with a half hour walk to the river for a baptismal service first. Once again, the country is so beautiful the walk was a pleasure. Eight people were baptized. Then, back to the church for singing (special singing and some not so special)—seemed like there would be no end. Since it was Thanksgiving, people brought some of their produce; there was a lot of vegetables and fruit. Someone even brought a goat.

There was a Thanksgiving Offering taken. It was a very large church, no walls just pillars, and it was packed, with another crowd of people all around the outside. They picked a man and a woman to "pass the hats," and it became a contest to see who would collect the greatest amount of money. The people spoke Creole, a language like French. Romeo could understand a lot of it, but I didn't understand any. All at once I realized everyone was looking at me and clapping—they had chosen me to be the woman to take up the collection. It was quite a challenge, because the

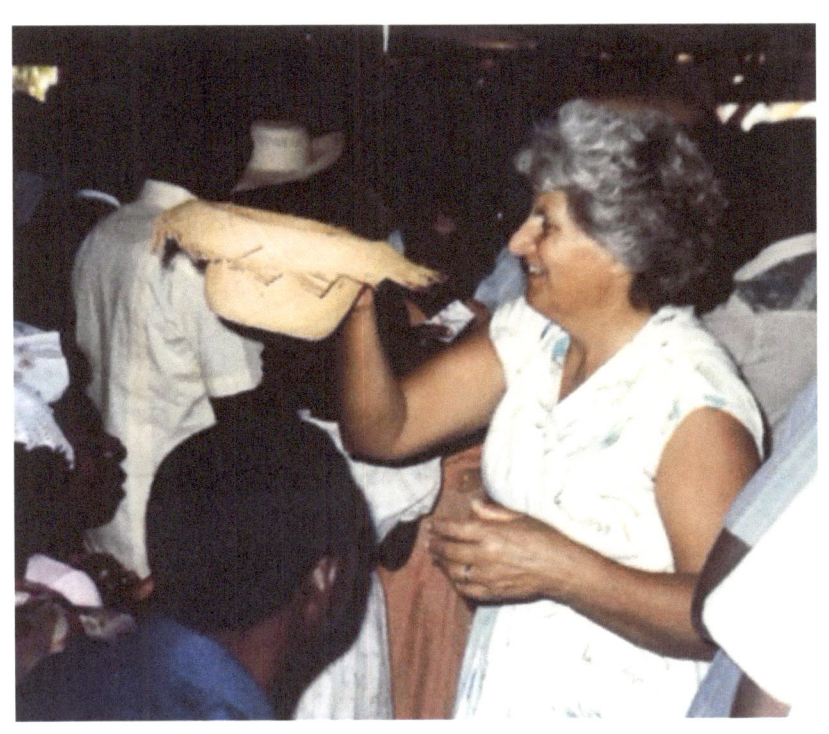

Top: Having been chosen to be part of a team to collect the offering at a service, Mary passes a hat among the congregation.
Below: Mary and Romeo have a snack at a Haitian home, before beginning the long walk home.

Top: Romeo works on a "floating foundation" for a building, in Haiti. Below: A shirtless Romeo tries to beat the heat of a Haitian sun, while building a wall for a new church in Port au Prince.

church was packed with people, and it was hard to move around. All the time the people were clapping and cheering us on. The man won with 155 goudre; I had 95 goudre. A goudre is equal to 20 cents, so it wasn't a lot of money by our standards, but for Haitians it was probably what they might expect.

The sermon wasn't short, and then there was a wedding ceremony. It's now 1:45 p.m. Are the ceremonies over? Not so. We walk a short distance to another house, and food is served. There were about two dozen guests to eat a meal of bean sauce served over rice and fried chicken. They don't waste any of the chicken; they use it all. Marg Brown, (missionary nurse from Stayner, Ontario), was sitting beside me. Marg wasn't sure but thought she was eating a chicken leg, until the top broke off. Marg realized it was the head and neck. After we ate, we still weren't ready to go—there was yet another wedding in another house. The minister, Steve Zurcher, who was with us, officiated at the ceremony. And then, finally, we were ready for our drive back to Zelda's. The sky was pretty black on our way home; we were praying that there would be no rain, because when the roads became muddy, they were impossible to drive on. We were all tired, and happy to get back to Zelda's, but pleased that we had attended the "service." It was a day—an experience—to remember.

Romeo always worked hard and fast, too much so for the good of his health. This was the case when he worked on the waiting-room building. There was a lot of cement work to be done and Romeo was carrying the cement from the mixer in large pails. One day he had a pain in his stomach, the next day was worse, plus, he noticed a lump. A doctor from the U.S. was there; he was organizing a team of doctors to come to Haiti to do work in Zelda's clinic, and Zelda asked him to examine Romeo.

The doctor's report—Romeo had a hernia, which meant no more work for him, and an operation as soon as we got back to Canada. We were lucky our flight home was only a week away. The job left to do was finish the floor. Romeo became just a boss and explained what was to be done while the Haitians and I finished the floor. Romeo didn't do anything after leaving Zelda's, so it was fortunate that our time was almost up, as he could only sit around so long.

The missionaries had planned a retreat by the ocean, before we left for home, and we got in on it. The Reverend Dennis Applebee was the guest speaker; he always had a good message, and he had a great sense of humour. For four days we worshipped, slept, ate, swam and snorkeled. Romeo and I thoroughly enjoyed snorkeling; we spent as many hours as possible just lying on the water, watching all the beautiful fish, coral and plant life in the ocean.

After the retreat, Romeo and I went with the missionaries to Port-au-Prince, and from there on to the airport next day.

Haiti 1990...

In 1990 we went to Haiti for the third time, this time for six weeks, from October to December. Most of the missionaries from the Missionary church had left Haiti; the twenty years they had planned for Haiti were finished. Only Marilyn McIllroy, from Palmerston, Ontario, and Sam and Cathy Berky, from the U.S., were there. Marilyn had asked Romeo and me to come for a visit, and Romeo said we would come sometime when there was some work to do. Sam and Cathy wanted a break, so they could go home for four weeks, and Marilyn wanted company while they were away, so Romeo and I decided to go for a visit. There was also work for Romeo.

To go to Haiti this time we decided to drive to Miami and leave our SUV in the Missionary Flight Airport. We left home with lots of time to drive to Miami and really enjoyed our drive. We drove down the east coast and by way of the 23-mile Chesapeake Bay Bridge Tunnel, which is very interesting. It is one of the seven engineering wonders of the modern world. Romeo was very impressed, and so interested he bought a book, telling everything about it. It was built so that ships could sail into Chesapeake Bay without having to deal with a drawbridge. It is also shorter than going around the bay by car.

After crossing the tunnel, you are still not on the mainland, but on an island still far out in the ocean. You take a ferry to another island and a second ferry to Virginia Beach (a city, also a county in Virginia), the mainland, and then you continue south. We spent time in St. Augustine, the oldest city in America. Romeo was interested in the structure and details of the old buildings.

Cathy and Sam used our vehicle while they were home. The plane we flew in belonged to the missionaries. It was an old Douglas DC3, the kind used in World War II. The plane held about twelve passengers, the actual amount varied depending on the weight of the passengers, plus their luggage. Passengers sat on one side, and the luggage piled on the other. The flight attendant would be anyone available. He would be chosen at the last moment and given a few instructions by the pilot just before take-off. A prayer was said before flight by the pilot, which could be taken two ways—make you feel good, or make you wonder, are they sure we will make it? The latter must have been on Romeo's mind, because when the flight attendant was closing the door Romeo asked, "Are you sure you got that closed right?" The reply was, "I think so. If not, I'm sitting up front with the pilot, and will be the last one sucked out." We flew to Cap Haitien, stopping in the Bahamas for fuel. I'm happy to say it was an uneventful flight.

During our six weeks in Haiti there was work for Romeo, including three gazebos to build. Romeo had Haitian men helping him, right from the cement floor to the woodwork of the roof. He helped build the wooden frames, and the Haitians put a thatched roof on them, which was made of palm branches.

We enjoyed our visit with Marilyn, who was living in the duplex we had helped to build when we lived in Haiti for six months. We lived with her during this third time in Haiti.

To come home, we flew from Cap Haitien to Port-au-Prince. At Port-au-Prince we waited four hours while they did some work on the plane. It was wonderful to view Haiti from the air; flying at a low altitude you could see the contours of the land with all the mountains. We spent Christmas in Miami. It rained Christmas Day, plus it was quite warm. With warm weather, no snow, Christmas there didn't appeal to us. Our thoughts were of Christmas in Canada. The next day, we were on our way home.

When we got to the Cove, cars were parked on top of the hill—too much snow. Romeo didn't feel like walking down the hill; with the 4WD, it wasn't a problem for him going down and driving back up when needed. Our neighbour, Bernice Langlois, was always amazed how Romeo could always drive up the hill when everyone else was "chicken." She told Romeo he must have "mountain-goat power" in the engine, instead of horsepower.

We only got stuck below the hill once, and that was because of ice. It was early spring, we were the only ones using a car for the hill, and we were doing okay. There was lots of slush and snow, and one night it froze solid. There was no way we could drive up the hill. Our good neighbours, Arnold and Bernice Langlois, told us we could use their car any time we wanted to get out, just stop for the keys on our way up the hill on our snowmobile.

One day Romeo (the great problem solver) had an idea. There was a pile of sand at the bottom of the hill, so Romeo put some in the sleigh behind the snowmobile and we went up the hill. While I drove down at a very slow speed, Romeo stood in the sleigh and shoveled two strips of sand far enough apart for the wheels of our SUV. The idea worked; Romeo had no problem driving up the hill.

The church at Kauai in 1986, (we were members of a Work Team)

The South Seas and South America

Kauai…
In January 1986, we went with a Work Team to Kauai. Our friends Edith and Emerson Hisey were also on the team. It was a big job, and would take more than a year to complete, with many teams contributing their efforts before and after our work tour. A church, educational building and a daycare centre were being built. Gene Cherry and his wife Janice were in charge. Gene had a very successful construction business. When he retired, he and Janice spent their time organizing volunteer work teams to build churches or whatever was needed, mostly for the Missionaries. Their home was in California, where they spent most of their time, but they also had a house in Kauai.

Romeo made his "mark" again, always hardworking, able to do whatever was asked of him. Gene was very impressed with the work Romeo did. With Romeo's work experience with Hydro, he didn't have to be told what was to be done or how to do it. We enjoyed Edith and Emerson's company plus the beautiful place to work, the swimming and the sightseeing tour we were taken on.

In 1991 Gene Cherry was in charge of another job, this time in Hawaii. Gene was pleased when he heard Romeo would be on the team, because Gene would be away part of the time and planned having Romeo take his place while he was away. However due to health problems (I had cancer that had to be taken care of), we couldn't go; we let Bruce and Pauline take our place. Gene was disappointed, as Bruce was a pastor, not a carpenter, and couldn't fill in like Romeo. We didn't know Gene's plans for Romeo, or we would have let him know Romeo wouldn't be there.

South America / Brazil / The Faws…
In 1986 Gene Cherry was asked to build a church in Brazil. He wanted the job done quickly, so instead of the task being open for anyone to volunteer, Gene picked experienced men he knew would be able to work fast. Gene phoned Romeo, who was ready to go. Then Romeo mentioned me. Gene said he wasn't including women this time, but Romeo said

he "didn't go on work teams without Mary." I was allowed to go. I was happy, as I didn't want Romeo to go without me.

It was a very long trip, with a two-hour stop in Miami, and a four-hour stop in Belem in the middle of the night. We had a quick stop in Manaus, then on to Porto Belho. By late afternoon, after a four-hour bus ride, we arrived in Ariguemes (where the church was to be built). The floor of the "to be" church was poured, and by the time the sixteen days were up the church was finished; Sunday service was held in it.

There was mostly cement block work to be done, except for the arch for the front entrance, plus trusses for the roof. Romeo was happy to do any of the woodwork, and since the arch for the entrance took some thought to complete, Romeo enjoyed the challenge. I liked to work with Romeo and often found chances to do so, but I was appointed to work in the kitchen. There were five other women in the kitchen: Janice Cherry; a missionary lady, who came with us from Porto Belho because she could understand English; and then the lady from the church with her two daughters. I wasn't very happy about the arrangement—it is easier to take the heat and living conditions if you are busy—but the situation changed soon enough. The man working with Romeo flew from Hawaii to meet the group in Miami, and then to Brazil, a very long flight. Unfortunately, on the second day he became ill. So, I got to work with Romeo, to take his place. There were always jobs for me when Romeo didn't need me, such as cutting re-bar for anyone needing a certain length.

This was the only Work Team we were on that we didn't like. Everyone except Janice took their turn at being sick. The only way to endure the feeling was to lie down on one of the pews in the old church, with a bag of beans or rice for a pillow, and moan or groan. If you were lucky, you might even go to sleep. Romeo was sick on the Sunday and didn't miss any work. We were a long way from the Amazon River, but where we were was considered part of the Amazon jungle. It was very hot and humid. The missionaries weren't really prepared for us. One thing they didn't have was bottled water, or any water that was safe to drink, so Janice would add some Javex bleach to the water to kill any germs. It didn't go down very well.

The missionaries in charge of the project, Ron and Jennette Faw, were both teachers. When they first came to Brazil to teach in the schools and also spread the gospel message when they could, their daughter Christa was only one year old. They had planned to stay in Brazil for one year. They stayed in Brazil till they retired, about 2016, and moved back to their home in Kitchener, Ontario. Christa is still in Brazil.

Ron and Jeanette lived in the same area (called Rondonia), and in the city of Ji Paranau. It was quite a distance, but Ron was at the site most of the time, even though he was in a wheelchair. Romeo liked Ron and told him if he ever had a project that he and I could help him with, we would come for a couple months. Nine years later, in 1995, Ron had a project. Ron phoned Romeo, would he come? Romeo had changed his mind and said we would come for two weeks. Ron reminded him he had said two months. Romeo couldn't say no, and in April of 1995, we were in Ji Paranau till June. The weather was quite hot, but there was very little humidity in Ji Paranau.

We lived with the Faws for the first month; the second month, we lived in a minister's house, while they were away on vacation. In Brazil, to prevent theft, one never leaves their house empty, even though they have high walls (with glass chips on top) and iron gates. We liked living by ourselves, buying and cooking our own food. Ron had lots of jobs to do, but the main job was making small tables and benches for little people. The tables were made with an angle on the ends—you could put two side by side and make a hexagon or put them end to end for a long table. If you put the angles together the right way you could make a round table with an open space in the middle. The tables were three feet on one side and four feet on the other side, making the angle. The benches were two feet long, and high enough to go with the table. We made forty-two tables and ninety-nine benches.

Before our departure to Brazil, Romeo had asked Ron if he needed anything; we would bring it with us when we came down. Ron had sent him a list, thinking that Romeo would pick out some of the tools, etc. We told the people at church about what we were doing and asked if anyone had any tools they would like to give toward the cause, or to give a donation so Romeo could buy some. We got a great response from our church family, and by the time we left Romeo had filled the whole list Ron had asked for. It was sure all worthwhile when we saw how surprised and pleased Ron was. "It's like Christmas," he said. "Two Christmases!" He was so appreciative of all the tools we brought, and for the work we did while we were there.

We enjoyed getting to know Ron and Jennette and their daughter Christa, who worked in the orphanage. Jeannette and Christa were in charge of the orphanage and had other women hired to help. One day Ron and Jennette dropped us off at an interesting young couple's place while they went on to do business somewhere else. This couple had three young children. We couldn't speak Spanish and they couldn't speak English or French. We had a lot of laughs trying to understand each other. Their name was Kennedy. I don't think we could pronounce their given names.

The Kennedys, in Brazil. Their only method of transportation was a motorcycle, and all five of them could fit on it!

Mr. Kennedy was a carver, and he gave Romeo a lesson. Most of the furniture in Brazil is carved; I'm sure Romeo wouldn't have any problem learning the trade. They gave us a sample of some freshly roasted meat. We were interested to know what it was, and by the picture they drew it looked like a pig. They called it a paca; it was wild. They caught it at night, shooting it as they rode a motorcycle, holding a flashlight on the running animal. It was delicious. The only transportation the Kennedys had was a motorcycle, and all five(!) of them fit on it.

While staying the last month at the minister's house, we had a problem. When the mail was delivered, we would just put it away, so we had no idea that two of the letters were hydro bills, requesting payment. One day, a man came to the large gate that was always locked, wanting in. Romeo, not knowing what the man wanted, let him in. The man walked right over to the electrical box and turned the hydro off. After he left, Romeo said, "I could just turn it on again." He didn't, though, which was smart, because he could have ended up in jail, and we were due to go home in a few days. We put in a miserable night, because we depended on two fans to keep us cool and to keep the mosquitoes away, but the Faws soon got them to turn the electricity on again.

We celebrated our 20th Wedding Anniversary while in Brazil. We had the Faws help us celebrate, and we chose a restaurant on the top floor of the highest building in Ji Paranua—the food there was supposed to be good. The tallest building was three stories high. The food was okay. We had a nice time.

Two months in Brazil made for special bonding with the Faw family, and a few years later the Faws were at our church in Lion's Head. Ron wanted to visit our home to see where we lived, even though it was winter, and he was in a wheelchair. Where there is a will there is always a way. We managed to get him in the sleigh behind the snowmobile and down the hill we went. We could drive right to the door with the sleigh and got Ron back in the wheelchair for use in the house. Ron was happy, so it was worth the struggle.

When the two months were up, we were happy to be going home, but definitely pleased we went.

Brazil, 1995. Romeo and Mary celebrate their 20th Wedding Anniversary, sharing the special occasion with Ron, Jeannette, and Christa Faw.

Ecuador…

In February of 1990, we joined a Work Team going to Ecuador. We flew to Quito on a Friday, but we wouldn't be leaving for Esmeraldas, where we would be working, till Monday, so we spent the time between shopping and sightseeing. Since beef is the cheapest meat, we all enjoyed a great meal of steaks or roast beef. We had a beautiful drive in the Andes Mountains. We saw the line marking the equator and the monument there, and, as is the custom, we all stood with one foot on either side of the equator line and had our picture taken.

Even though Quito is near the equator, the temperature is always between 60 and 78 degrees. This comfortable temperature is due to the high altitude. In Esmeraldas, where we worked, the temperature was usually 100 degrees. It was right on the ocean. The flight to Esmeraldas took three-quarters of an hour in a small plane. Because we flew low, it was a beautiful sight over the Andes to the ocean. From Esmeraldas it was an hour drive to where we worked.

While there, we stayed in cabins right on the ocean and ate in the restaurant there. The food was very good, lots of fresh fish. There were three women on the team. We had to make breakfast (an eye-opener, due to all the cockroaches, though we soon got used to them). We also had to make sure the men got all the water they needed and do the laundry. The work site was a twenty-minute walk from where we lived. We carried water from the camp where we lived, and the laundry was done at the work site.

The work for the men was building cement-block cabins for a children's camp. There were twelve bunks to a cabin, also toilets and sinks. With hundred-degree temperatures and high humidity (not like Quito), it wasn't a pleasant job. At the end of a hot day, it was nice to think of taking a refreshing dip in the ocean, but the ocean was as warm as bath water, not refreshing.

There were fifteen members on the team, and we were there for twenty days. We went back to Quito by bus, which was a beautiful drive through the mountains, but hard on the nerves—sharp turns, deep valleys and no guard rails. The speed driven was very fast, and since there were lots of potholes, they drove all over the road. You just kept telling yourself, "You are safe, nothing is going to happen." That night, on the front page of the newspaper, there was a picture of a bus that didn't make it.

In Quito we still had one day of pleasure. We visited a farm which was part of the virgin jungle. It was an interesting tour, but we only had three-quarters of an hour. We also ate in a restaurant by a lake that was situated in what had been a volcano. Interesting, because no one had ever gotten to the bottom.

Our nineteen days in Ecuador, working and sightseeing, proved very interesting and rewarding.

The Dominican Republic...
February 23 to March 9, 1993, was our last mission trip. It was to the Dominican Republic. The work was to paint and do odd jobs in the guest house. This is where the missionaries lived and where we stayed while there. Romeo was in charge of the work. Edith and Emerson from our church were on the team. Edith and I worked together; we painted three

bedrooms, four bathrooms, the dining/living room, kitchen, and laundry room.

Repairs had to be done on the roof, and a garbage bin was made. Romeo also made a bed for the teenaged chore boy, Richard, who was sleeping on the floor. Everyone enjoyed Richard, he was a real comic, and he entertained us in the evenings.

We often talked about our "work team days," and of the many other workers, some very interesting ones. We looked back on fond memories and we were so happy that they were part of our lives.

CHAPTER 5

Travels

When Romeo was working (and a few times after he retired), we spent time in Florida. These times while Romeo was still working were always in November, after the cement work that needed to be done was completed. After November it was too cold to pour cement. Romeo took most of his holidays at this time, so we would spend three or four weeks in Florida. After we moved to our home at the Cove, we had water right in our backyard and beautiful summers. In winter we had our skis and snowmobiles, so we really didn't need Florida.

North American Road Trip…
Romeo and I had a very interesting and full life together. As well as Work Teams, we did other trips.

After Romeo retired, we planned a motor-trip in March 1987. Our plan was to go across the Southern States, up the West Coast, and home through Canada. In Texas, at a nice camp called Big Bend, we set up our tent for the first time. It was also the last time we would use it. Romeo set up the tent, we had supper and went to bed. I was wakened in the night by a strange noise. It was Romeo. I tried to wake him and realized he couldn't speak or move, and that he was sick. I rolled him over on his side and he threw up. By morning he was still sick, but he could once again speak and move.

When we were leaving, we told the lady in the office about what had happened to Romeo during the night. She suggested Romeo take an aspirin and a Coke. She said his illness was caused by the water. "There is so much oil in the ground that the water isn't good to drink. It will make you very sick but won't kill you." We hadn't seen any signs warning people not to drink the water.

I took the tent down and stored it in the vehicle, where it stayed for the rest of the trip. I also did the driving for the day, which wasn't far, to Carlsbad Caverns, in New Mexico. By evening Romeo was feeling much better and was ready to eat. We checked out the caverns the next day and then drove on to the West Coast.

We visited Gene and Janice Cherrie on our way to San Francisco. Gene had been the leader of some of the Work Teams we were on. We enjoyed some time in San Francisco. As we rode the trolley, we were reminded of the television show *The Streets of San Francisco*. We started walking across the Golden Gate Bridge but had to turn back when it began to rain.

We travelled north on U.S. Route 101, along the Oregon Coastal Highway; it was beautiful all the way.

Portugal…

Romeo heard from a friend that Portugal was a good place to go for the winter months. Temperature warm enough but not too hot. Since it was off-season it was very reasonable pricewise. In 1997 we went for two months and were pleased. We went to the Algarve area, which is on the southern coast, on the Atlantic Ocean.

We left on Romeo's birthday, January 19. The Bruce Clark family met us near the airport, in a Swiss Chalet restaurant, to celebrate his birthday. Pauline brought a Black Forest cake (Romeo's favourite), which she left in the kitchen, with instructions on when the waiters were to bring it to our table. They brought it to the table while singing "Happy Birthday" to Romeo. Romeo was pleased. The cake was delicious. We had a great time.

We stayed at Praia da Rocha, in the Algarve region. A twenty-minute walk along a path through bush and rock took you to a little town called Portimao. It was a delightful walk, and we did it many times. Portimao was quaint, with its narrow streets and old buildings. Romeo was interested with the structure and details of the buildings. We found an English restaurant, which we visited more than once, that served wonderful fish and chips, also steak and kidney pie, both our favourites. We enjoyed Portugal but didn't go back till 2014, and again in 2015, staying for one month each time.

The first two times in Portugal we had apartments with kitchens, and we made a lot of our own meals. It was good exercise to walk one kilometer to the large store to buy groceries. Romeo and I like fish, and there was lots there, of different kinds—many we had never heard of. The last time in Portugal, we didn't have a kitchen; a wonderful buffet breakfast was included with the room, and we ate other meals at different restaurants.

Europe by Bus…
We did a thirty-five-day bus tour of Europe, visiting thirteen countries. The trip was very interesting and enjoyable. We saw lots and heard lots, far more than we could ever remember. Some of the highlights of the trip were—the cruise on the Rhine River, in Germany; the beautiful scenery, especially the Alps; beautiful Lake Lucerne, in Switzerland, with the cogwheel train taking us up the mountain. Around the halfway mark there was a plateau with a building and some grazing cows. It reminded us of the story, Heidi.

We had a free day in Rome, which we made good use of. Romeo was interested in seeing the aqueducts, which he had read about, plus the Pantheon, so we decided to do a walking tour. We got a map that showed us where to go and what we would see and took a taxi at 9:00 a.m. to the furthest attraction, which happened to be the Pantheon. Romeo was so excited. "Imagine," he said, "I'm standing in it, the place I've always wanted to see!" Romeo was really amazed at the huge dome on top, with no supports except the walls. The nuclear reactors Romeo worked on during his last years working at Hydro, though not as massive, were built in the same manner. It was 6:00 p.m. when we finished the tour, ending up back at our hotel. We had seen a lot and were tired, but very pleased with our day.

A Caribbean Cruise…

In the late 1970's we went on a two-week cruise, with nine island stops, in the Caribbean. We met, enjoyed, and became good friends with the couple that shared our four-person table. The gentleman was John Meston, who wrote scripts for the television show Gunsmoke, and his lady Mary Anne, who had a television show also. John was very interested and intrigued with Romeo and his stories. John said he could get lots of ideas for his show, listening to Romeo.

Mary Anne liked to drive, so they always rented a car and invited us to go with them. We saw a lot of the islands. When it came to driving, Mary Anne seemed to like a challenge. Nothing would stop her, any kind of car or gear shift or "wrong side of the road"—she was up for it! We enjoyed the rides, even though they could be a bit "hair-raising" at times. One day, driving through beautiful country and steep gorges, the motor stopped while Mary Anne was turning a sharp corner and at the same time ascending a steep hill. Mary Anne took a little while (too long!) to get the motor started; in the meantime, we were inching our way backward to the edge of the gorge. Mary Anne was quite cool about the whole ordeal, while we three sweated it out. Another time Mary Anne came too close to the curb, and the result was a flat tire. The timing and place weren't good, as we were quite a distance from the ship, and there wasn't much time before the ship was to sail. We did make the ship on time, and Romeo didn't "thumb his way" as he had threatened.

Mary Anne and John became very special to us and added much enjoyment to our cruise. John and I corresponded for many years. They invited us to visit them in California. We didn't visit them but often wished after that we had. Finally, John's letters stopped, and later we saw his name in a paper, connected with a death. John's name was referred to as "the late John Meston." We were sad, we always had fond memories of John and Mary Anne.

Facing page, top: Romeo and Mary on their first cruise in the Caribbean. Bottom: We share a table with John and Mary Anne Meston, while on a cruise in the Caribbean. John wrote the scripts for Gunsmoke, a popular television series, and was convinced that he could use some of Romeo's stories as ideas for the show.

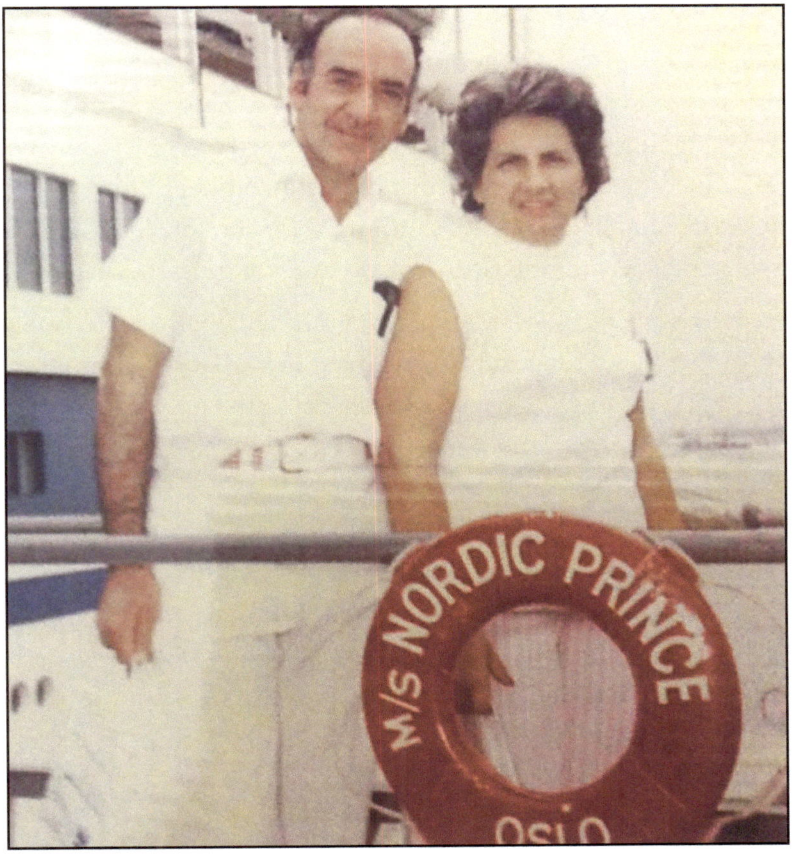
M/S NORDIC PRINCE
OSLO

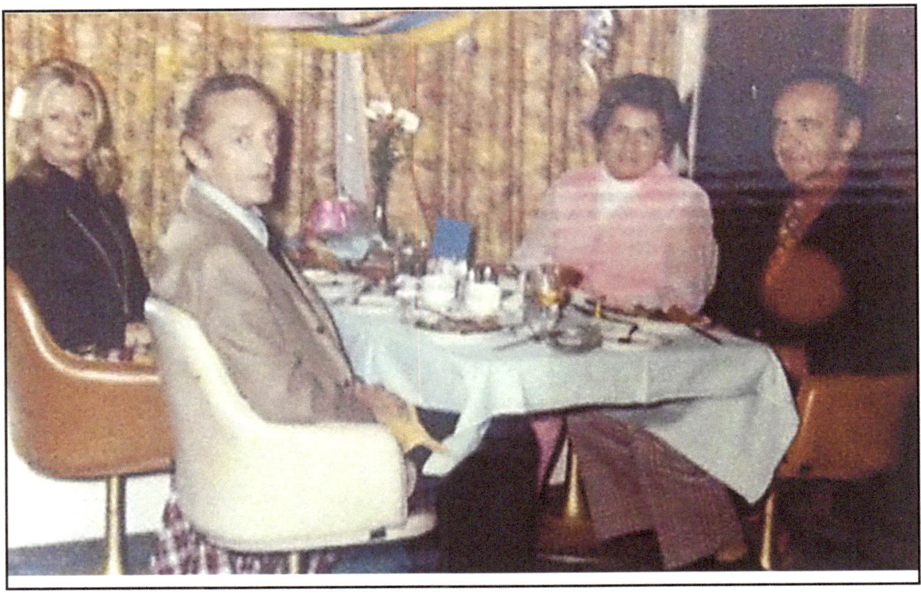

Antarctica / A Cruise in the Southern Ocean...
Our last cruise was to the Antarctic, in 2006, for three weeks, over the Christmas season, December 21 to January 11. The ship was well-decorated, including many Christmas trees—everything festive for the season. We sailed from Rio, not sure of the temperature, but it was hot. We started with shorts, the farther south we went the cooler it got, until we were wearing our winter coats when we were on deck.

The water was very rough by the Falkland Islands, so bad we couldn't sail between the islands, as had been planned, just went by them. The boat was rocking so much one could hardly walk, the pool was closed because of the waves in it. The water continued this way till past the tip of South America.

The cruise was scheduled to go as far south as Petermann Island, but due to the narrow passage, the loose ice and the wind, it was considered too risky, as the ship might get frozen in the ice. When this danger was explained, there were no complaints about not going farther. We were told of a ship being frozen in so solid they had to bring an icebreaker from Russia to free it.

Twelve scientists from Palmer Island made their way to our ship in Zodiacs (rubber dinghies with outboard motors). Our captain was expecting them, for this was a yearly get-away for them. They stayed for the whole day, enjoying the pool, the hot showers, and all the delicious food they wanted. The scientists gave us a talk on their work, the reason why they lived in that part of the world.

Palmer Station was the farthest south we went. By now it was the second day of January, just past the longest day of the year in the Antarctic. The temperature was minus six degrees (this being the summer season, it was probably the warmest it would get), with sunrise at 2:52 a.m. and sunset at 11:57 p.m., which made for a very short night. We turned around in a little bay which wasn't much wider than the length of our ship.

Heading north we passed through the rough water again. The waves—fifteen to twenty feet high—continued until we reached the tip of Chili.

L: Romeo celebrates the first day of 2006, at a party on a cruise ship bound for a three-week cruise in Antarctic waters.

Below: Well-dressed residents of the Antarctic region, a pair of penguins pose for a picture.

Massive icebergs float on the horizon. On a cruise in the Southern Ocean, our ship was advised to stop heading south - we ran the risk of being trapped in a sea of ice.

Sailing up the west coast of Chili was called the Inside Passage; it was a continuous sail through straits, channels, and canals, and protected on both sides by the lower end of the Andes Mountains. It was very beautiful, with waterfalls and glaciers among the mountains.

We docked one more time at Punta Arenas, Chili, where we took the shore excursion to see the penguins. There had been lots of penguins farther south, sitting on floating ice around the huge icebergs, but from the deck we were too high up to see them, and, unfortunately, we had forgotten our binoculars. The tour was an hour-long bus ride and then a twenty-minute walk to see them, all well worth the effort. The penguins are fascinating, walking around in their "swallow-tailed coats," and posing to have their pictures taken (or so it seemed). There were fifty or more of these interesting creatures, we obliged and took lots of pictures. Our cruise ended at Valparaiso, Chili. From there we were taken by bus to Santiago, where we took our flight home.

Dominican Republic / Fruits of our Labour…

As part of the celebrations for Romeo's ninetieth birthday, we spent a month in the Dominican Republic. This was our last trip together, because I thought it too risky for two people in their nineties to travel alone. We were blessed to never be sick on any of our trips, never enough to use our health insurance, except in the Dominican Republic. Romeo was sick, but he didn't think it serious, and we went to a Pharmacy for the pills he always takes for what he thought was this familiar illness he gets. We met Dr. Donais Nester there, a very pleasant Dominican man, who told us he wouldn't give Romeo pills without examining him first. The doctor found something wrong and said that Romeo should go to the hospital. He phoned for an ambulance then helped me contact Sun Life Financial, our health-insurance company. I was having problems with the call—first I couldn't hear the gentleman, then I didn't understand him. Dr. Nester took the phone and argued for a while with the man at the other end of the line. Then he said, "This man is sick. He has to go to the hospital, and he can't wait till tomorrow for your answer!" After a short pause the doctor said, "Thank you very much." We had no further problem with the insurance coverage. As we prepared to leave in the ambulance, the doctor said, "I want to hear from you when you return."

While examining Romeo, the doctor had asked him if we had been in the Dominican Republic before. Romeo told him of our Mission trips, and how we had been to Dominica once before, on a Work Team. Dr. Nester went on to say that if it weren't for people like us, he would not be a doctor. "We were given clothes," he said. "My schooling and my university training were paid for." He was so thankful and appreciative it gave me goosebumps just listening to him.

Romeo had an infection in his stomach, so we stayed in the hospital overnight, remaining there until the next afternoon. Returning to the resort, we saw Dr. Nester. He asked if they treated us well, and if they fed us. We told him yes, on both counts, and he said, "They don't usually give you food, but I told them to treat you well, because you are my parents." This was a good joke, for the doctor was black and we are white. Later, when it came time to say goodbye, I thanked him for the help he had given us, but he replied that it was he who should thank us. He then gave us his email address and asked us to let him know if we got home okay.

The Tours to the Holy Land…
We went on three memorable tours: two to Israel and the Holy Land, and one to Turkey and Greece—which included a cruise around the islands, following in the footsteps of the journeys of the apostle Paul. Our first tour to the Holy Land, in 2010, was with the People's Church in Toronto. Pastor Charles Price and his wife Hilary led the group of over four hundred people. Bruce and Pauline were part of the group. They had been blessed with tickets provided by the collected efforts of their church, former churches where Bruce had served, and friends and family. The occasion for the gift was Bruce's 65th birthday, and the recognition of his forty years (in 2009) in the ministry. Bruce suggested Romeo and I should join them on the trip, and we were pleased to go.

We flew to Egypt, landing in Cairo. While there, we viewed the pyramids, and found ourselves—along with everyone else—asking the usual question: How was it possible to pile such huge blocks of rock, each weighing one or two tons, using only manpower? For tourists, it was the thing to do, so the four of us decided to try riding a camel. A camel is pretty high off the ground, even when lying down, and though it's simple for younger people to get on one, it's not so easy for older folk. Still, it was probably more of a challenge for the owner of the camel, as he had to help us into the saddle. We also visited the Cairo Museum, which is a large building, and with Romeo's interest in history, the time spent there wasn't long enough for him.

From Cairo we travelled by bus—thirteen of them! —across the desert to Israel and the Holy Land. It was a privilege and a blessing to visit the Holy Land, to walk where Jesus walked, to see where He was born and grew up. When we came to the place in the Jordan River where He was baptized, we viewed some people from another tour group watching from the shore as some in their group were being baptized. The onlookers were singing and praising God.

Always up for a new challenge, Romeo takes a ride on a camel, in Israel.

Because our group was so large, we were all together only a few times; one such time was in the Garden of Gethsemane, where Pastor Charles held a service, Hilary Price was the speaker, and communion was served. It was a very special and meaningful event. The trip itself was special, made even better by the amount of time we were able to share with Bruce and Pauline.

Our second trip to the Holy Land, in 2013, was with the Rosewood Church of the Nazarene. Billy and Shirley Perryman, our friends and neighbours, were also on the tour. Just as we had done on the first tour, we flew to Cairo, but this time we went through Jordan as we made our way through the Holy Land.

After leaving Cairo, we were offered an option to climb Mount Sinai to watch the sunrise. This had also been included in the agenda on the last tour, but we four had declined. We realized after that this had been a good idea, for it was a strenuous climb, starting at 1:00 a.m. and returning by 8:00 a.m. This trip, quite a few people decided to take the option, including Billy Perryman. Some of them couldn't make it to the top and the group didn't all get back till 10:00 a.m., two hours later than scheduled. This put the entire schedule behind—there were other things to see, including the place where Moses saw the burning bush, before we moved on. Because we didn't have time for the usual beautiful buffet lunch, they made box lunches that we could eat on the bus. As our bus drove through the desert, we ate what they had prepared for us, and like the Israelites of old, who complained about their manna, there were some grumbles. The food was a far cry from the buffet we had expected!

Shortly after crossing into Jordan, we came to the remains of one of the Seven Wonders of the World, the very interesting and unbelievable Petra, an ancient city partly carved out of the high walls of rock surrounding its location.

We followed the eastern shore of the Jordan River, and this time, some people from our group were baptized. Though this visit to the Holy Land was much the same as it had been on our first trip, the experience was just as special and meaningful as it had been the first time.

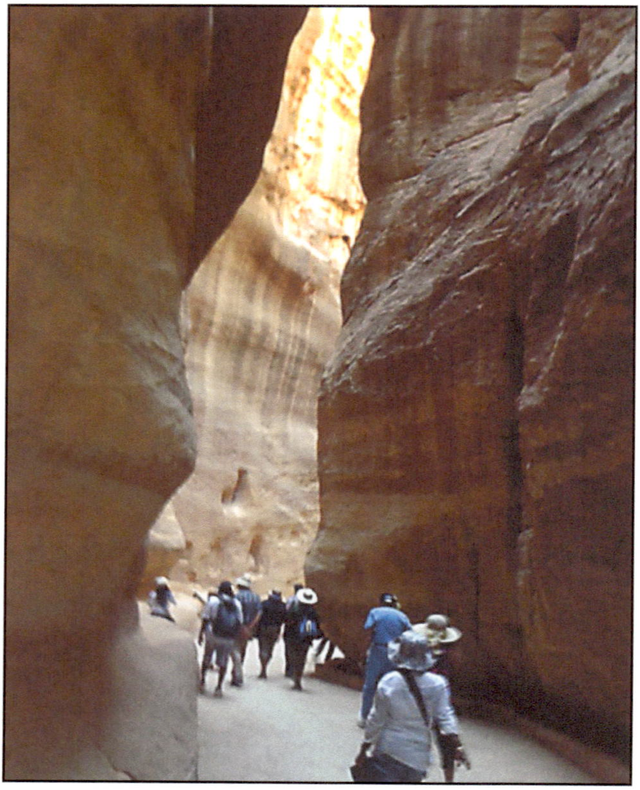

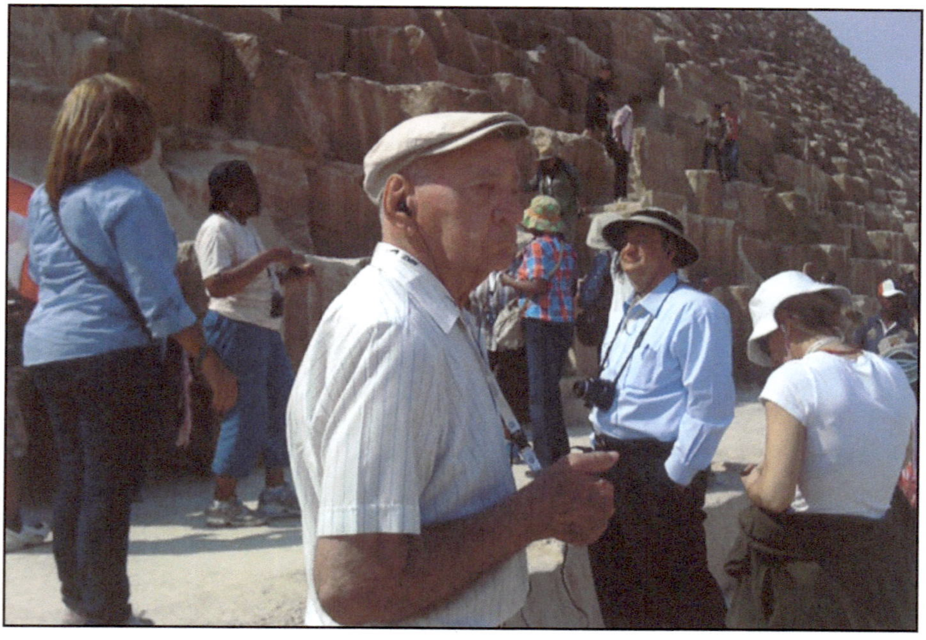

The third tour was with the People's Church to Greece and Turkey, again with Bruce and Pauline. We flew to Istanbul (ancient Constantinople), in Turkey. Romeo was disappointed, as we didn't see much there. He had read about the city and was looking forward to seeing more of it.

We spent two days in Turkey, flying to the southern coast and viewing the areas with the remains of the seven churches Paul had started when he journeyed there. Bruce was especially interested in these locations.

From Turkey, we cruised the Aegean Sea and the Mediterranean Sea to Greece, sailing among the islands, visiting where Paul travelled and planted churches. We didn't have much time left for Athens and a bus trip where we saw the Corinth Canal. The canal was interesting—so deep and narrow, just wide enough for a ship. We flew home from Athens.

Romeo and I enjoyed the trip, even though it was too much for us. We couldn't keep up the pace and missed out on a lot. We were fortunate to have Pauline and Bruce with us, to fill us in on what we missed.

When we got off the plane in Toronto and walked up the long ramp to the airport, we didn't refuse a ride on the trolley, which had been waiting for people like us. The trolley left us off at an elevator where an attendant was ready with two wheelchairs. I assured her that I was okay to walk, and that I would be able to push my husband. The attendant put us on the elevator, and we were right in the luggage section of the terminal when we got off. Bruce and Pauline were soon there to take over and put us on our bus to go home to Port Elgin.

Facing page:
Above: On the path to the ruins of the ancient city of Petra, in Jordan.

Below: Romeo visits the Great Pyramid in Egypt. He had a love for architecture, and was always interested in construction techniques. .In this photo, it's easy to imagine that he's hard at work, figuring out how many tons of stone were needed to build the gigantic structure!

Romeo and Mary visited Portugal thrice, in 1997, 2014 and 2015.
Top: Our hotel in Portugal was right on the beach. From the balcony to our room, Romeo could take in the sight of the sun, the surf, and the sand, while enjoying the brisk ocean breeze.

Below: Romeo reads a book while relaxing on a tranquil beach in Portugal. He had given some thought toward writing a book about his own life, while he vacationed in Portugal, but, after some discussion with Mary, he decided to shelve the idea and just enjoy the vacation.

The Yukon in our Van…

In February of 1994, Romeo and I decided we would like a visit to the Yukon (the land of the midnight sun), especially Dawson City. Having picked a destination, we faced the decision of how we wanted to travel. We didn't want to stay in motels; our favourite way was to camp, but our tent-trailer was long gone.

One day, in Owen Sound, we saw a large cargo van (it was more than long—it was one with the extra length). The thought occurred to Romeo that it could be used as a camper. We checked it out, only five years old and in very good condition. The price was right—only $6,000—so, we bought it. Since the van was white, with the owner's business printed on the door, Romeo got it painted a nice shade of red. The van was also very noisy when driving because it was empty. Romeo soon fixed that, by putting a sheet of plywood on the floor, and lining the walls and ceiling with carpeting. This made a great difference.

Since we would be sleeping in the van, we needed a bed. We found some good bed springs at the dump, but later realized they were only three-quarter-sized; we wanted something more comfortable—full-size springs. One nice Sunday, a beautiful day for a drive, we just happened to pass by another dump. Since it was Sunday and the dump was locked, we parked the van and walked in to check out the site, in the possibility of seeing the right size of bed springs. We saw exactly what we wanted. That Monday we decided to get rid of our undersized springs, so we went back to the dump with the full-size springs. When the lady in the office asked us what we were leaving, Romeo said we were dumping off some bed springs. The lady gave him the okay, and he backed up to where the springs were, the van blocking the view from the office. Romeo pushed out the old springs and loaded the full-sized ones, which were in good condition, and just what we wanted. We were pleased and left the yard with a little less junk. Too bad these dumps waste so much by not letting people take things they can use. I'm sure the lady in the office would be happy if she knew about the switch, and how much it meant to us.

Romeo built a frame for the springs to sit on, making it just high enough for Knob Hill Farms' boxes to fit under it. (Could anything be handier, than just putting your clothes in a box and pushing them under the bed?) We also had a folding table and chairs in the van. There was still space to store the many other things that one needs while camping.

Romeo thought of the mosquitoes we would have to deal with, since it was June, and not being able to open the van windows at night meant that it might get pretty warm. He bought some mosquito screening and fastened it around the window with Velcro. It worked fine, it was easy to put on and take off (we didn't leave the screen on during the day). We realized how important those screens would be, on the first night, after we set up for supper and the blackflies found us. We made record time heating wieners and beans, eating supper, and cleaning up!

The price of the van was $6,000; add $1,000 in costs for the paint job and to line the vehicle with carpet—we paid a total of $7,000, which wasn't much to pay for a comfortable "camper." Plus, after the trip, Romeo used the van to transport lumber and the furniture he made, until his days doing shop work came to a close. No longer needing the vehicle, Romeo sold the van for $1,000 to a couple who made trim for the woodwork in houses. It was an ideal work vehicle for them, as they needed the length. They used it for many years before it finally gave up.

On one of the many happy trips we took in our faithful little camping trailer.

As an aside story, the little tent-trailer we used for camping (before we owned the van), which had served us so well and given us enjoyment for so many years, deserves a better ending than that it was "long gone." True, to us it was long gone, but when we got rid of it, little did we realize the trailer still had many years yet to go.

My son Doug heard Romeo say the trailer was ready for the junk yard; there was a leak in the roof which Romeo couldn't seem to stop. Also, we were living in our house by the Bay, and who needs to go camping when you have everything right in your backyard? Doug and Marianne (with their three little girls—Ruth, Mary and Sarah) decided they could use it, so on our next trip to Alberta we delivered the trailer. Doug managed to seal the leak, and they used it for camping. At home, it was used as a playhouse by the girls, and a fun place to sleep in. This went on for many years, till the girls grew up. Again, the trailer looked like it was ready for the dump, so it was parked behind a building, out of sight. There it sat, but not completely empty, for some mice found it ideal for a nest.

Doug and Marianne McCulloch and their three daughters – (l to r) Mary, Ruth, and Sarah – warm themselves at a hearty campfire. Doug and his family made good use of our little trailer, after Romeo and I decided it was time to give it up.

Time went by, the girls became adults, and Mary's husband, Zach, saw the trailer and decided he could make use of it. Doug was glad to get rid of it (and the mice!). Zach stripped it down to not much more than the box. He put larger wheels on it and added a hitch, so it could be pulled behind a four-wheeler. The little trailer saw a lot of use around the farm, and not only for work, because their four children also enjoyed rides in it.

Driving to Dawson City…

We stopped to visit my son Doug McCulloch, his wife Marianne and their girls, in Barrhead, Alberta. Passing through Whitehorse, we spent some time with my nephew Alan Hansen, his wife Sonya, and their boys. In northern BC we took a break in Liard River, where we enjoyed the Hot Springs. While in the Whitehorse area, we visited Skagway, read lots of information about the gold rush, etc. Alan drove us around, taking us to see some of the historic sights: Lake LaBerge, mentioned in the Robert Service poem, The Cremation of Sam McGee; the huge and interesting Dredge No. 4, about 14 km outside of Dawson City; and the monument marking the discovery claim that started the gold rush in 1896.

The scenery on the drive to the Yukon had been beautiful, but to me the highlight of the trip would be the chance to see the midnight sun, in Dawson City. This, however, was not to be, because even though we stayed in Dawson City for five days, it was cloudy the whole time. Still, it was an interesting stay. We visited the house that Pierre Berton grew up in when his family lived in the Yukon. We watched a film, where the writer spoke of his childhood days spent in Dawson; he mentioned his grandfather, a man who was around during the Gold Rush, when the White Pass (part of a route to the gold fields) became known as 'Dead Horse Trail,' because 2,000 horses died on the rough road over the mountains. We also went to Robert Service's cabin, where we listened to a recitation of his well-known poems, read by a local resident, Tom Byrne.

Alaska, Vancouver, Homeward…

It was a beautiful, scenic drive from Dawson City, on the 79-mile long 'Top of the World Highway' to Tok, Alaska. Very slow driving, with hairpin turns, but high enough to be near the snow on the mountains. We turned south from Tok, still high in the mountains, to Haines where we took a ferry to Prince Rupert and on to Vancouver by Prince George. All beautiful country—breathtaking, with the mountains, and the views along the Fraser River.

In Vancouver we spent some enjoyable time with Romeo's son, John, and his wife Maureen. They took us to Granville Island, very interesting—and we wouldn't go to Vancouver and not walk the seawall in Stanley Park. We continued to enjoy the beauty of the land as we drove through the Rockies to Calgary, where we stopped to visit my daughter Bonnie and her husband, Peter.

Finally, after our stay in Calgary, we turned our steps homeward. It was a great five-week trip, exploring the Yukon, even if I didn't see the midnight sun in Dawson City.

Home Again, Our Special Place…
Romeo and I did a lot of travelling together, and we enjoyed the many places we visited; felt blessed, and fortunate, for our experiences—but our special place, the place where we appreciated life the most, was at home.

Romeo Enjoyed Young People

Left: Romeo and my grand-daughter, Sarah McCulloch.

Below: The Birthday Boys! David Clark (my grandson) and Romeo whoop it up during one of the birthday celebrations they enjoyed together. Though separated by years, their birth dates fell in the same month, just three days apart.

Below left: My grand-daughter, Ruth McCulloch, removes a fresh loaf of delicious bread from an outdoor stone oven she designed and built.

Below right: Ruth's son, Jesse McCulloch, tries his hand at baking.

Top left: Romeo hugs Sarah McCulloch.
Top right: Two generations enjoy a good book. Romeo with Mary's great-grandson, Caleb Kennedy. When the great-grandkids came along Romeo and Mary became Père and Gigi.

Right: Abigail Bouchard (Mary's first great-grand-daughter) has a special smile for a not-so-secret admirer.
Below: "What's so funny?" Romeo would crack people up with this simple question and a straight face.

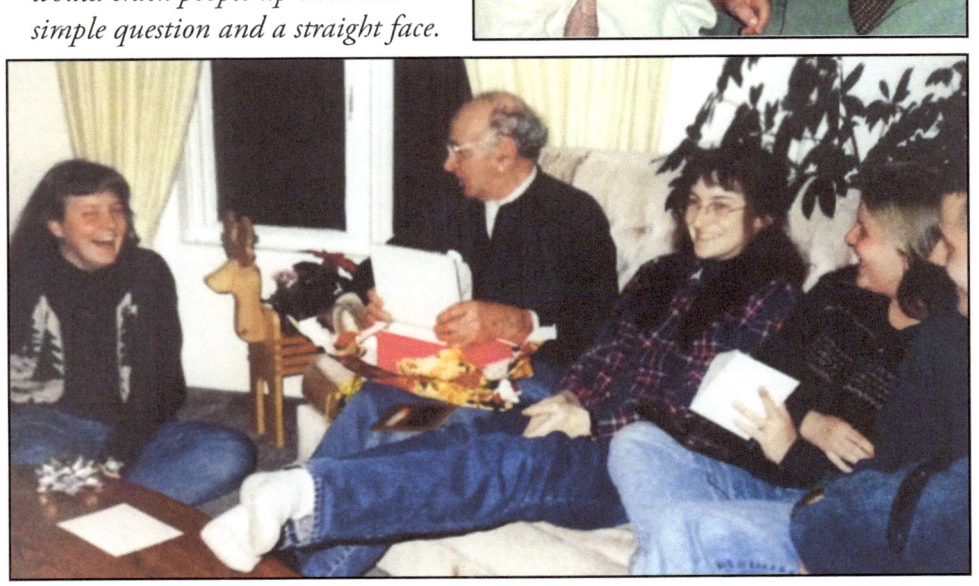

Above: I'm surrounded by Mary (my grand-daughter) and her husband, Zach Olthuis, and their children – (l to r) Kate, Danica, Levi, and Reese.

Below: My daughter Pauline and her husband, Pastor Bruce Clark (front row, centre), surrounded by family at the grand celebration of his 75th birthday/50th year of ministry, June 2019.

Above and left: My daughter and her husband Peter Clark in Canoe BC, where Bonnie is savouring retirement after many years as a swimming instructor and Peter continues to delight audiences as a professional musician in the Okanagan.

Below: My son Doug McCulloch and his wife Marianne with their three daughters and their families in Barrhead, Alberta, where Doug and Marianne have been apiarists for 45 years.

God's Healing Touch

The Bible says God numbers our days before we are born. God not only gave Romeo and me a lot of days, but He also gave us good days, with very little pain or sickness. Most of our ailments were minor, or the result of an accident: Romeo broke an elbow when he fell on some rocks in his early years with Hydro. Though I've never broken a bone, I fell off a horse and dislocated an elbow when I was ten years old. In his late teens, while he was lifting a section of the rack for his truck which was far too heavy for one person to lift, Romeo felt something give, and that "something" bothered him for a long time. Some days he would have to miss work, the back pain would be so bad.

In the late '70's, Romeo told his doctor in Oshawa about the injury. Dr. Kingsman told Romeo to bend over and touch the floor. Romeo did so, and whatever that action told the doctor, Dr. Kingsman knew the remedy. He felt that leg exercises would help solve the problem, and he gave Romeo three different leg exercises, to be done every morning. Romeo followed the doctor's instructions faithfully—he did the exercises every day for the rest of his life, and he never had another back pain, even when he did the heavy work of building our house.

Romeo and I both liked the winter months; the snowmobiles made great ski trails, and we did a lot of skiing with friends and neighbours. The hill near our home was perfect for tobogganing, and with the snowmobile to pull you back up the hill, it couldn't get better: "older" children, grandchildren, the Hill family and other friends—all enjoyed the fun of flying down that long, steep hill. At 73, I knew I should have been past that stage in my life, but one day when Doug and Marlene Hill and family were visiting, I couldn't resist. The kids wanted to go tobogganing; their parents didn't want to go with them, so I decided to take one more ride down the hill. It was in March, there wasn't much snow, and what little there was of it was hard and packed. Flying down the hill, I put my foot out to help steer. My foot caught in the snow and my leg bent at the knee—the wrong way. I injured three ligaments. After the doctor put them right, he mentioned to me that in three or four years I would probably need a new knee. Well, my knee was fine—no pain—and I have no doubt it will be with me to the end.

Some health challenges, however, were more serious. We both had our brush with cancer. It was 2006 when Romeo was diagnosed with prostate cancer. He needed radiation treatments for seven weeks, which he had in the Kitchener Waterloo hospital during March and April. It made sense for us to rent an apartment in Kitchener for the duration of the treatments. The hospital was trying a new plan to accommodate more patients, so he got a double dose of the radiation every other day, instead of daily; none on weekends. Thank God it worked! The cancer never came back.

I had a malignant tumour removed from my bladder. Later, because my family doctor thought it looked like the cancer was coming through the lining of the bladder, I had some CAT scans done over the next few months. When it was finally clear that it was coming through the bladder, I was scheduled for an operation to remove the bladder. I have great faith that God can and will heal if it is His will. I also believe He will help us through bad times in our life. I prayed for God to heal me if it was His will. Most of all, I prayed for God to help me accept what I had to go through and give me peace.

The peace God gave me, was beyond my imagination, and He healed me—the doctors found no cancer. After the operation, as I was coming back to "the real world," I had an overwhelming feeling of joy. It must have been noticed. I heard a nurse say, "She is still smiling."

In 2007, Romeo narrowly survived a heart attack. We had been in Toronto, delivering a piece of furniture Romeo had made for a friend of Bonnie's. We also visited Bruce and Pauline. It had been snowing quite a lot while we were gone, and a lot had accumulated in our driveway. Once again, when a job had to be done, Romeo puts all he's got into it. He started shoveling, and this time it was too much. He came into the house complaining of a terrible pain in his chest. He took his boots off and went straight to his room. I wondered what I should do. Should I take him to the hospital? I went to ask him what he thought. One look at him and I already knew. His face had turned grey. I phoned 911 immediately and in 10 minutes the ambulance was at the door. Two girls came in and in no time, they had Romeo on a stretcher with an IV started in his arm. At the hospital, the doctor told us that 15 minutes later they couldn't have saved him. The next day Romeo was taken to St Mary's Hospital in Kitchener where he had an angiogram done. One artery was 90% blocked and the other not quite as bad. He needed two stents. The ordeal started Sunday and by Wednesday Romeo was home again. I was sure glad to have him back! Romeo rested for a few days before he was back in his shop, in our basement. Once again, we thank God for the quick action of those paramedics and the doctors knowing what to do. Romeo had no problems with his heart after that.

Mary enjoys a visit with Romeo at the nursing home on Valentine's Day 2019

God's Amazing Grace

It's quite clear in the Bible that we don't earn salvation by our good works: Christ made the supreme sacrifice when He died on the cross, making a way back to God for all humanity. The way of salvation was explained to Romeo by several people, including a very dear friend, Jim Byrnes, who was filling in at the Baptist church in Port Elgin until they got a permanent pastor. Anyone who talked woodwork and showed interest in his shop was a friend of Romeo's. Jim was interested in both, so he and Romeo would spend lots of time in the workshop whenever Jim and his wife Dolores (a beautiful person whose company we also enjoyed) came to visit.

As I have said before, Romeo had great faith in God and definitely believed in prayer. He spent a lot of time in his room, especially after he retired. Romeo liked history and read a lot of James Michener's books. He also read his Bible, and the devotional books he got every three months from the Catholic Church. One of Romeo's favourite books was the story of John Newton, who wrote the hymn Amazing Grace—which was his favourite hymn; he asked his granddaughter Bonnie to sing it at his funeral.

I was so happy when Romeo came out of his room one day and told me that he had surrendered his life to Christ. I had made the same decision in 1979, and never regretted it. I first heard the way of salvation when I was about ten years old. For some reason I didn't understand, when I would pray, I didn't get the response I expected. Still, I always thanked God, because as long as I had that desire to know Him and to be accepted by Him, I thought He would still call me. He hadn't given up on me. I wanted to know God, truly know His love, have Him make His home in my heart. This went on all my life, till 1979.

One Monday night, back in our Oshawa home, after Romeo had gone to bed, I sat up late, reading a good book (*Beyond Ourselves* by Catherine Marshall) and crying out to God in prayer. Again, I didn't get the response I expected. On Wednesday, as always, I went to Mt. Albert to help Pauline clean, or to do whatever she needed help with. While there I got this feeling which I can't explain—it went from the top of my head right through my whole body to my feet. At the same time, I felt exceedingly joyful, and I knew for sure that God was giving me the response I seemed to need before I could truly believe He had forgiven my sins and accepted me as His child. When I shared my experience with Pauline she was overjoyed. She told me she had stayed up late the same night as me, praying for my salvation. I knew she had been praying for me longer than that. Pauline's relationship with Christ began just a few years before, through the help of the NCF group (Nurses' Christian Fellowship) and particularly her roommate, Sonja Lane (now Barfoot). This was while she was training for her RN certification in Owen Sound. Although I didn't record the date, I know that I too have been born again into God's family, because of His promise in I John 1:9 that whoever comes to Jesus in repentance, He will forgive.

The last photo of Romeo, taken at the retirement home by Pauline, two weeks before his passing. Though frail, he still had his sense of humour. When Pauline mentioned she'd never seen the scar on the back of his head, Romeo replied with "Neither have I."

CHAPTER 6

Romeo's Passing

Our life together was good, except for the last three months. More than a year before, Romeo was diagnosed with dementia and it was getting worse. It was thought that caring for him was getting to be too much for me, but it was so sad to think of putting Romeo in a nursing home—he didn't want to go, and he never did get to like life there. But Romeo didn't complain, and he even said he realized it was too much work for me.

To take Romeo out of our home and put him in a nursing home was the hardest thing I ever had to do. We both shed many tears over the decision, and to make it worse, it didn't end up well. Less than two months later, Romeo had a fall in his room, tripping over a mat lying on the floor by another resident's bed. He fell on his back, hitting his head so hard it caused internal bleeding. After the fall, he couldn't walk, and had to use a wheelchair.

Four weeks later, my dear Romeo passed away. As he had requested, Bonnie, with her siblings Julie and Sonja, along with their mother Pauline, sang Amazing Grace at his funeral.

I thank God that someday we will meet again to sing God's praise together, and that can't be too many years away.

Amazing Grace

Amazing Grace! How sweet the sound
That saved a wretch like me!
I once was lost but now am found;
Was blind, but now I see.
'Twas grace that taught my heart to fear,
And grace my fears relieved.
How precious did that grace appear
The hour I first believed.
The Lord has promised good to me;
His Word my hope secures.
He will my shield and portion be
As long as life endures.
Thro' many dangers, toils, and snares
I have already come.
'Tis grace hath bro't me safe thus far,
And grace will lead me home.
When we've been there ten thousand years,
Bright shining as the sun,
We've no less days to sing God's praise
Than when we'd first begun.
~ *John Newton*

Memory Lane

Romeo's ninetieth birthday was approaching, and so was the question, "What do you do for, or give, someone who is ninety?" Pauline and her daughter Bonnie thought of putting together a Book of Memories. The following are some of the memories and tributes for Romeo on that occasion, left by friends and family who knew and loved him.

Mary Heroux

In conversation with (left) Michelin (Romeo's niece/Real's daughter) and Agathe, his sister

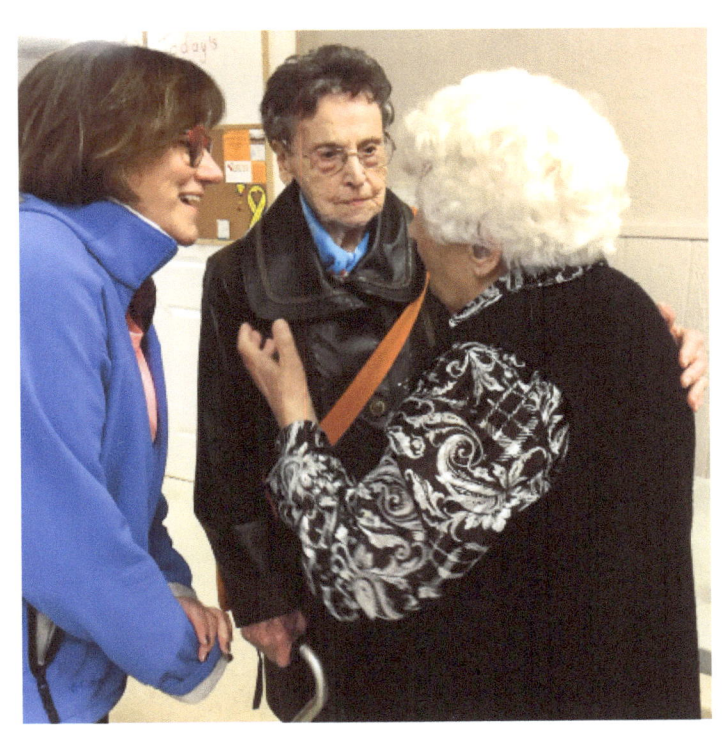

JOHN L. HEROUX
(Romeo's son)

It was one of those bitterly cold days in Little Long Rapids. Although the sun was bright and there was no wind, it was freezing—below-freezing cold. It must have been the weekend, and Dad was taking me along for the ride in his Hydro truck to Harmon, or to Kipling. In those days we weren't able to drive home (we had to take an old train north from Kapuskasing), but there was a construction road that went north from Little Long to the other two dams, at Harmon and Kipling, passing through Smoky Falls. Anyway, as we were driving along, we came upon a First Nation woman who was probably walking from the train station to the Cree camp up the road, near Woboose Creek. She was carrying packages—probably after having shopped at Little Long or Kapuskasing.

Dad pulled over to pick her up and give her a ride. As she was climbing in the back of the open pick-up truck, I was probably staring off and daydreaming. I must have been thirteen or fourteen at the time. Dad looked at me and asked, "What are you doing?" I didn't know what he was talking about. He told me to get myself out and into the back of the truck and let that woman sit in the front where it was warm. "What if that were your mother?" he asked. "Would you let her sit in the back?"

For the next little while I had the chance to think about it while I froze. He was absolutely right. That wasn't the way we were raised—and I should have known better. I was proud of my father, that day, for showing me to do what was right.

ANNE MARIE HEROUX
(Romeo's daughter)

At my wedding, in 1975, after the reception when the hotel owner brought the bill, my Dad said, "I don't need my glasses for this. Just put my hand over the signature spot and I'll sign."

At Romeo's funeral in Mattawa, Ontario:
Above: left to right: Maureen, Anne Marie and Doug Bell, John Heroux, who was ready to give his tribute to his dad.

Below: right to left: Anne Marie, Bonnie Kennedy, Marianne McCulloch, Sonja Russell

CLARAN MARTIN
(One of our Pastors in Lion's Head)

We have appreciated your friendships over the years, after we got to know you and Mary, while we pastored in Lion's Head. I always enjoyed our conversations about all kinds of topics. I was so proud of your diligence in seeking to be a blessing on all the mission trips you went on, the things that were done to help others. It was a joy to see you perfect your carpentry skills and see the amazing things you were able to build with your hands. Thanks for your love and care for us over the years, we always felt very supported by you.

LORNA COOK
(niece)

First, I want to say thanks for being such a wonderful uncle. When I look around our kitchen, living room, the bedrooms, rec room—every room, I see you! The stimulating conversations we always had… Hydro career, and what you accomplished there—the hundreds of men you have supervised… Memory highlights, perhaps, our visits at the Cove—fresh air, sunshine, and lots of laughs.

KELLY COOK
(great niece)

My first woodworking experiences were with Uncle Romeo—making a television cabinet, in his shop, for my Grade 8 Wood Shop project.

MARY OLTHUIS
(Granddaughter)

I knocked over the Christmas Tree in a game of Blind Man's Bluff and was feeling terrible. Grandpa cheered me up in his gruff way, saying he was sick of that stupid tree and the mess the needles were making anyway. Time for it to come down. My girls play with the doll's bed, table, and chairs you made for me. Levi uses the breadbox Grandpa made for a tractor shed. Another memory is Grandpa dancing with my girls at Sarah's wedding.

BONNIE KENNEDY
(Granddaughter)

So many great memories during my years in university. I always loved meeting up with you and Grandma in Toronto. Lots of interesting dinners along Yonge Street, especially Marche. I'll never forget your dismay as the bill kept adding up! The many times you moved me from one place to another—I had my own private moving company!

JULIE BOUCHARD
(Granddaughter)

Memories—Slicing up turkey at countless turkey dinners, making triple-bunk beds for our Cabbage Patch dolls, when Sonja and I were ten. Skidoo rides down to Jackson's Cove (some pretty lively ones). Loved when you would reminisce about your younger years—your laugh is pretty happy too. The rocking horse you made, first dreaming up an idea for a more practical kitchen, then making the cupboards (What a beautiful kitchen!). Coming to Long Lac for Christmas—the special bond developed between you and little Serenity. Stewart's mom and aunt and you singing in French (or trying) had us all laughing. Many many times over the years you have been the life of the party.

SONJA RUSSELL
(Granddaughter)

Grandpa you are a man of strength and intelligence, hard-working, diligent, and persevering. You are so neat and organized. You have built countless pieces of beautiful furniture for all kinds of people including each one of our family. We are privileged to have your mark in our homes. The house at the Cove you and Grandma built is beautiful—love the big windows, the skylights. The wonderful smell walking into your shop, Grandpa. It's neat to hear you and Grandma reminisce of past times with us.

RUTH McCULLOCH
(Granddaughter)

I recall a bit from when Grandpa and Grandma came to help Dad get the honey house in our yard cleaned (after our parents bought it). Particularly burning the grass! I remember Grandpa teaching me to eat peanut butter and honey mixed together right off our large-sized soup spoon. Also remember at Niagara Falls and Marine Land, I think it made him sick watching Grandma and I, on the rides. Also remember Grandpa at the Cove, whipping up a nice wood frame for one of my completed Christmas gifts. It was an ugly little craft but sure looked good in an oak frame.

RUTH CLEMENT
(friend)

Carl and I loved going to Romeo and Mary's and bringing our friends there. We all loved Romeo's sense of humour. Carl was amazed at Romeo's workshop and tools and when he saw the canoe Romeo made, he was totally blown away.

MARILYN McILROY
(friend)

Romeo (and Mary) have been part of my life since the beginning of my career in Mission work in Haiti. It was such a blessing when Romeo put the steel roof on the Medical Building. Romeo often remarked about the necessity of using mahogany trusses (very expensive, but the only wood available). I often remarked that Romeo was "the only Romeo in my life."

BONNIE (& PETER) CLARK
(My daughter)

A fun time with Romeo and Mom was while staying with them over Christmas Holidays, in their condo in Oshawa. We walked from their place on a beautiful snowy New Year's Eve to Mother's Pizza and had a wonderful pizza. Also, the driving trip with Romeo and Mom to Louisville, Kentucky, in 1992. We really looked forward to it after the trip with them a few years earlier to Nashville. We were delighted and surprised that they were willing to take us again on this trip.

THE GAMMIE FAMILY
(Friends from the Cove)

One of our first memories of Romeo was of him using that great yellow steel sleigh to help us get in and out of the cove with our gear. He never spared the throttle on the snowmobile! When we finished building our house at the cove we were in a bit of a predicament for furniture. Romeo's passion for and love of building high-quality wood furniture was known to us by that time. One piece at a time, we put in an order and each in turn was finished in the shop at the Cove, with later pieces added after Romeo and Mary moved to Port Elgin. Over the space of a few years, we acquired a house full of fine oak furniture, thanks to Romeo's skill and hard work. The harvest table in our kitchen has developed a fine patina over the years and, like Romeo, it holds many memories.

RON (& JEANNETTE) FAW
(friends)

First time we met was in Ariguemes. You and Mary were on another Work Team, to build a church. Next time was in Ji Paranau, you and Mary came and brought me a new drill and other tools. It was like Christmas. You built chairs, and forty-four tables, for the orphans. Then the visit to your home on the Bruce Peninsula. The ride down the hill in the sleigh behind the snowmobile in a storm, a wonderful time. I got to see your shop and the canoe you were making. You impressed me in so many ways.

JACKLYN COOK
(Great-niece)

I have a few great memories of Uncle Romeo. I remember all the summers at the Cove. Romeo taught us how to use the lathe and all the aspects of his shop. Also, how to skip rocks. There was so much fun.

PAULINE CLARK
(My daughter)

Every day, as I walk through our home, I see beautiful one-of-a-kind pieces of furniture that are a constant reminder of all your hard work, your talent, and your creativity. The beautiful hutch—a replica of an antique I admired in a friend's home, oak frames, coffee and end tables to suit our smaller space, oak table and chairs. Bunk beds for the girls (three had to share one room), miniature bunks for their Cabbage Patch dolls. Of all the things you made us my favourite is my desk, with bookshelves above.

BRUCE CLARK
(Pauline's husband)

When we moved to Thunder Bay, in the townhouse there was no Study. You flew—flew Friday after work to Thunder Bay, and in whirlwind fashion you put up a very functional Study and flew back to work on Monday. It was very thoughtful of you, and very much appreciated.

DAVID CLARK
(Grandson)

Remember Grandpa showing me how to run his snowmobile and letting me take it when I was twelve. Watching Grandpa in his beautiful workshop. Hikes on the Bruce Trail, but especially when he took Heather Miousse and me down a short cut from the Bruce Trail down the cliff. Everyone else went the long way.

My Romeo
Romeo Heroux

---

a life remembered

Romuald 'Romeo' George Lucien Heroux

19 January, 1926 — 28 April 2019

A Last Word…

During the process of writing my book I was asked, "What is your most precious memory of Romeo?" I have so many good memories of my time with him, it would be hard to choose the most treasured one. I can't easily tell you what I most remember, but I can tell you what I miss the most about my Romeo: his sincerity.

Romeo seldom gave a compliment, unlike those people who are "full of them." When Romeo complimented me, I knew it came straight from his heart, and I loved it when he gave me a compliment.

I hope he likes this book, because I wrote it as a compliment to him.

Mary

"When I consider Your heavens, the work of Your fingers,
The moon and the stars, which You have ordained…"
[Psalm 8:3]

Acknowledgements

I am thankful to the following people. Without you, I couldn't have written this book.

Anne Marie Heroux and Maureen Maloney (Romeo's daughter and daughter in law). You are the ones who told me I should write a book of Romeo's life, as a tribute to him, since he always wanted to write a book about his life. I wouldn't have even started this book if you hadn't insisted that I was capable of the task.

Pauline Clark, my daughter. You approved of what I had written when you read it, after I had been writing for a few months. At that point I had been wondering if I would even finish the project. Your continual words of encouragement after that kept me going on other occasions when I was ready to give up. Above all, I appreciate your patience with the many hours spent in editing and proofreading the manuscript and the book layout. Your connections with various people got the wheels in motion for the manuscript to become a book in print.

Brian Crum Ewing, my "creative consultant." You were still willing to assist me with my manuscript even after Pauline showed you a sample of my work. Your untold hours of typing up and editing my entire manuscript. On top of all that, your helpful suggestions and positive attitude were a source of never-ending encouragement to me—even though mostly at a distance, due to the pandemic restrictions of meeting together.

Cheryl Antao-Xavier, who designed the book layout and arranged for the printing and distribution of my book.

Above all, I am thankful to my Lord and Saviour, Jesus Christ. Any ability I have to write a book, at my age, and for the first time, comes from You. The memories I have recorded remind me of Your faithfulness. You were there, all the time, using our various life experiences to draw us to Yourself.

Lightning Source UK Ltd.
Milton Keynes UK
UKHW050222200821
389155UK00001B/3